D1617131

THE LETTERS OF MALCOLM LOWRY AND GERALD NOXON

DEAR RON & CAROL,
MANY thanks fr a
fabulous Winter 1994
Edmonton extravaganza —
every day a treat —
LOVE
Paul
(AND
HILDI)

Gerald Noxon (l) and Malcolm Lowry outside Noxon's
house in Niagara-on-the-Lake in March 1947

THE LETTERS OF MALCOLM LOWRY AND GERALD NOXON
1940-1952

Edited and with an Introduction by
PAUL TIESSEN

Assisted by Nancy Strobel

THE UNIVERSITY OF BRITISH COLUMBIA PRESS
VANCOUVER 1988

This book has been published with the help of a grant from
the Canadian Federation for the Humanities, using funds
provided by the Social Sciences and Humanities Research
Council of Canada.

Canadian Cataloguing in Publication Data

Lowry, Malcolm, 1909–1957
    The letters of Malcolm Lowry and Gerald Noxon,
1940–1952

    Includes index.
    Bibliography: p.
    ISBN 0-7748-0287-1

    1. Lowry, Malcolm, 1909–1957 - Correspondence.
2. Noxon, Gerald - Correspondence. 3. Novelists,
English - 20th century - Correspondence. 4.
Authors, Canadian (English) - 20th century -
Correspondence. I. Noxon, Gerald. II. Tiessen,
Paul, 1944–   III. Strobel, Nancy. IV. Title.
PS8523.087Z545 1988   823'.912   C88-091033-X
PR9199.3.L68Z489 1988

International Standard Book Number 0-7748-0287-1
Printed in Canada

*"I send you my love and when the tide
comes in and brings you some offering
try to pretend it comes from me."* (GN)

*"You are undoubtedly one of the best friends
and indeed one of the only real friends I have."* (ML)

CONTENTS

ACKNOWLEDGEMENTS

I gratefully acknowledge the kind permission and support of Margerie Lowry, Gerald Noxon, the Humanities Research Center of The University of Texas at Austin, the Special Collections Division of The University of British Columbia Library, and Peter Matson of Literistic, Ltd. in the publication of this correspondence.

I am grateful, too, for help from Ellen S. Dunlap and her colleagues at the Humanities Research Center, Anne Yandle and her colleagues at The University of British Columbia Library, Jane Fredeman and her colleagues at The University of British Columbia Press, as well as Frederick Asals, Andrew Berczi, John Chamberlin, Viviana Comensoli, Howard Fink, Alice Frick, Eva Hodgson, Bob Janzen, Marg Janzen, Margaret Linley, Russell Lowry, Fletcher Markle, Dave Mathews, Mavor Moore, Sheila Moore, Miguel Mota, Court Noxon, Janet Noxon, Pam Noxon, and Art Read.

Wilfrid Laurier University provided me with travel grants to interview Margerie Lowry and Gerald Noxon, and to examine the original letters in Austin and Vancouver.

For her assistance in the research and writing of the introductory and other editorial material in this volume, I am grateful to Nancy Strobel.

Paul Tiessen

CHRONOLOGY

1909

Clarence Malcolm Lowry born July 28 at Warren Crest, North Drive, New Brighton, Cheshire.

1910

Gerald Forbes Noxon born May 3 on Elgin Avenue, Toronto.

1915-1927

Lowry attended Braeside School, Wirral, the Caldicote School, Hitchin, and the Leys School, Cambridge.

1914-1926

Noxon received earliest schooling in Toronto; then, following war-time crossings of the Atlantic, attended schools in Europe, including public school at Stowe in England.

1927-1929

May-October 1927: Lowry went to sea as a cabin boy aboard the *S.S. Pyrrhus*.

Winter 1927-28: studied at Weber's School of Modern German, Bonn.

1928-29: lived in London, began writing *Ultramarine,* and began correspondence with Conrad Aiken.

Spring-Summer 1929: journeyed to America via the West Indies to meet and study under Conrad Aiken.

Fall 1929: entered St. Catharine's College, Cambridge.

1926-1928

Noxon travelled on the continent, spending most of his time in Paris, attending the Sorbonne and improving his knowledge of Russian, French, and German film, and of French and Italian language and literature.

Fall 1928: entered Trinity College, Cambridge, and became founding "publishing-editor" of *Experiment*.

1929-1932

1929: Lowry submitted a short story, "Port Swettenham," to *Experiment*, thereby beginning a series of visits with its editor, Gerald Noxon.

1930: travelled to Norway in an attempt to meet Nordahl Grieg.

1932: graduated from Cambridge with third-class honours in English; lived in London and Paris.

1928-1931

1929: Noxon became founding president of the Cambridge Film Guild and film-review editor of the weekly paper, *Granta*.

1930: introduced by Lowry to Conrad Aiken.

1931: graduated from Cambridge with an honours degree in French language and literature.

1933-1940

1933: in the spring, Lowry travelled to Spain with Aiken and Aiken's second wife, Clarissa Lorenz, and met Jan Gabrial; in the fall, Lowry's *Ultramarine* published by Jonathan Cape.

1934: in January, married Jan Gabrial in Paris; experienced problems with marriage; in the fall, followed Jan to New York for reconciliation.

1935: stayed briefly in Psychiatric Wing of Bellevue Hospital and, shortly thereafter, began writing *Lunar Caustic*.

1936: in the fall, travelled with Jan to Los Angeles and Acapulco; settled in Cuernavaca and began writing *Under the Volcano*.

1937: Jan left Lowry, who spent Christmas in jail.

1938: Lowry returned to Los Angeles and, despite considerable personal tumult, worked on a revised draft of *Under the Volcano*.

1939: began third draft of *Under the Volcano*; in early June met Margerie Bonner; was taken in late July by his father's legal representative, the Los Angeles attorney Benjamin Parks, to Vancouver, where he was joined in late September by Margerie; from October to the following summer carried on desperate correspondence with Aiken, in hope of moving into his household on Cape Cod.

1940: in late July sent third draft of *Under the Volcano* to his agent, Harold Matson, in New York, where a number of publishers in turn rejected it; moved with Margerie in mid-August to a rented squatter's shack in Dollarton, was notified by Aiken that Noxon had just moved from England to Canada, and immediately initiated correspondence with Noxon; divorce from Jan finalized November 1; Lowry and Margerie married December 2.

1931-1940

1931-32: Noxon was an editor of the monthly film review of the International Institute of Educational Cinematography in Rome, but left over a dispute involving Mussolini's use of the Institute as a political tool.

1932-40: worked in a variety of positions in London involving radio and film production, often for the BBC and for John Grierson's documentary film units.

1933: married American painter Betty Lane in London.

1940: returned in late summer to his native Canada.

1940-1944

Lowry wrote most of the fourth draft of *Under the Volcano* at Dollarton.

1940-1944

1940-41: Noxon worked under John Grierson again, now at the National Film Board of Canada.

1941-44: worked with the CBC, first (in 1941) on the *They Fly for Freedom* drama series, then (in 1942-43) on the *Our Canada* drama series and (in 1943-44) on the *News From Europe* documentary series; on CBC research and writing assignments in western Canada, Noxon visited the Lowrys at Dollarton in 1941, 1942, and 1943.

1944: began more serious radio-drama writing after Andrew Allan moved from Vancouver to Toronto to head the CBC drama division; worked at the same time on his own poetry ("Branches of the Night") and fiction (*Teresina Maria*) manuscripts, which he sent to the Lowrys for their criticism.

1944

June 7: the Lowrys' shack burnt to the ground; among the manuscripts lost in the fire was "In Ballast to the White Sea," among those saved was *Under the Volcano;* in July, having settled in with the Noxons in Oakville, Ontario, Margerie went for a few days to New York to discuss her own work and *Under the Volcano* with Harold Matson.

1944-1946

1944: in June Noxon wired money to the Lowrys so they could come to his home in Oakville, near Toronto; the Noxons moved from Oakville to Niagara-on-the-Lake in late summer and were joined there by the Lowrys on October 1; Noxon at work on a new novel, "Clegg's Wall," as well as several radio dramas and series for the CBC.

1944-1947

October 15: the Lowrys moved from the Noxons' Niagara-on-the-Lake house to a nearby rented house of their own.

Christmas Eve 1944: Lowry announced to the Noxons that he had finally completed *Under the Volcano*.

February 1945: after over seven months in Ontario with the Noxons, the Lowrys returned to Dollarton, and began building a new cabin.

June 1945: sent the new manuscript of *Under the Volcano* to Harold Matson.

November 1945: travelled to Mexico.

January 1946: after defending his *Under the Volcano* manuscript in a remarkable letter of literary analysis to Jonathan Cape, Lowry tried to take his own life in Mexico.

April 1946: *Under the Volcano* accepted by Jonathan Cape in London and Reynal and Hitchcock in New York.

May 1946: the Lowrys returned to Dollarton after having been deported from Mexico.

December 1946: travelled to Haiti.

February 1947: attended the public launching of *Under the Volcano* in New York.

1947-1950

Noxon dramatized *Under the Volcano* for radio in New York, with Fletcher Markle; further established his reputation as drama writer by adapting several of Conrad Aiken's works, including "Mr. Arcularis," for the CBC *Stage* series; moved to Boston to teach in the School of Public Communication (Film Studies and Broadcasting) at Boston University.

1947-1950

March 1947: the Lowrys visited the Noxons in Niagara-on-the-Lake and then returned (Malcolm first, Margerie a few days later) to British Columbia.

November 1947: sailed to Europe.

January 1949: returned to Dollarton and, in the months following, worked on a variety of stories, novels, and the film script "Tender Is the Night."

1950-1952

Noxon and his wife, Betty Lane, divorced; Noxon remarried while continuing his teaching career at Boston University.

1950-1952

Lowry worked on novels, short stories, and poems, and in 1951 mailed a 50-page statement to Harold Matson describing his massive project, "The Voyage That Never Ends"; Harcourt, Brace, who had bought the option on Lowry's contract, initially advanced funds for his project, but then dropped their option; in the spring of 1952 Albert Erskine, his old editor at Reynal and Hitchcock, now at Random House, provided Lowry, at least temporarily, with a contract.

1952: the Lowry/Noxon correspondence ends. Lowry left Canada in 1954 and died in England in 1957.

INTRODUCTION

The eighty letters and other messages published in this correspondence between Malcolm Lowry and Gerald Noxon offer an altogether fresh introduction to the life of Malcolm Lowry. In fact, it is an introduction presented as a kind of dramatic narrative, with a beginning, middle, and end of its own. It is marked by the writers' overtures to each other and definitions of their respective roles at the start, by nostalgic recollection and deeply-felt assessments of their relationship at the end, and by detailed expressions of past, present, and even dreamed-of future successes and failures, pleasures and disappointments, in between.

There are, of course, so many Malcolm Lowrys by now—those minted by biographers and critics, playwrights and novelists, film-makers, poets, and other readers. Malcolm Lowry "himself" established many of the biographical myths and legends now bearing his name. In this volume we are shown a Lowry made possible through Lowry's friendship with his old college pal, the Canadian, Gerald Noxon. Though Lowry himself was co-creator even of this particular identity, we inevitably come to regard it as Gerald Noxon's Malcolm Lowry.

Malcolm Lowry was born in England in 1909; he died there in 1957. However, during most of his adult life—after his undergraduate years at Cambridge University from 1929 to 1932 and the publication of *Ultramarine* in London in 1933—he remained abroad. In the 1930s he roamed about and lived, often miserably and grimly, almost always alcoholically, in Spain, France, the United States, Mexico, and, in 1939-40, Vancouver, Canada. Then, from 1940 to 1954 he lived for long periods in a series of rustic shacks in a wilderness idyll outside Vancouver. There, from August 1940 to June 1944—in a world into which he imme-

diately drew Gerald Noxon—life was for him unusually happy and
serene; he wrote well, drank little, and wandered not at all. But after June
1944, when a fire destroyed the shack which he had purchased in the fall
of 1940, his tranquility, inner and outer, again came under siege. Surrounded by Noxon's hospitality in Ontario from July 1944 to February
1945 he did manage to put the finishing touches on *Under the Volcano,*
which was published in 1947. But the years from the fire to his death
were marked also by several of his major manuscripts left incomplete, by
increased drinking and, again, a wandering—in Mexico, the United
States and Haiti, in continental Europe and England, and in Canada.

The letters, telegrams, and cards in this correspondence—a correspondence produced mainly by Lowry and Noxon, but also by Margerie
Bonner Lowry, Lowry's second wife—were written from 1940 to 1952,
and take in at length the hey-day of Lowry's early Dollarton period
(1940-44). Their strong narrative structure and drive carry us from those
early years, years of Lowry's most pleasurable and fulfilling creativity
(though even here not without making us aware of the pain and frustration of the years just before, or of grim horrors that even then seemed
capable of threatening Lowry's peace of mind), to the later years of
Lowry's valiant hope but little evident success. At the same time they
give us views of the two writing careers closely intertwined with his and
vigorously championed by him in the 1940s: Gerald Noxon's and
Margerie Bonner Lowry's.

Even though so many of Lowry's letters have already been published
elsewhere, this correspondence is replete with surprises. For one thing,
the present collection—with its plenitude of sensuous details describing
the initial Dollarton years, from August 1940 to June 1944—dramatizes
a period which, oddly enough, has so far been presented only in bare out-
lines elsewhere. In the 450 pages of Lowry's *Selected Letters,* only about
eight pages—only four letters, with none at all from 1943 or 1944—are
from that early four-year Dollarton period, during which Lowry was able
to write so well while, self-consciously Thoreau-like, he created for himself, for once, a romantically calm and relatively controllable home of his
own. Published biographies give us only sketches of the Lowrys' self-
imposed isolation on the inlet beneath the mountains at Dollarton: of the
Lowrys' contact with a handful of people there—with Whitey and Sam,
the fishermen who were their neighbours in winter, with Percy Cummins, the store-keeper close at hand, and with the magician who came to
visit; of Lowry's splendid physical form in those years, when he was
swimming several times a week; of his brilliant creativity as, sustained
daily by his wife (whom Noxon has described as having "salvaged" the

often self-destructive Lowry) as typist, reader, and editor, he battled *Under the Volcano* into the form that was finally published in London and New York in 1947. Lowry's short story, "The Forest Path to the Spring," is so far one of our fullest guides to the excesses of tranquility and peace of that period. The present correspondence recreates with immediacy, in the words of the actors themselves, the drama of those years.

Secondly, with Gerald Noxon—hitherto the shadowy "lifelong friend" mentioned sporadically in biographies of Lowry—springing to life in these letters, no longer will we base our impressions of him only on his passing appearance as one of Lowry's editors/publishers during his and Lowry's two overlapping years at Cambridge. No longer will Noxon—who was intuitively able to form a long and mutually accommodating relationship with the sometimes difficult Lowry—stand in simply as the good-humoured and long-suffering host opportunely at hand in Ontario when the Lowrys' shack burned down in 1944, or when the Lowrys were returning to Dollarton in 1947 following the New York festivities accompanying the publication of *Under the Volcano*. Here—in such contrast to the *Selected Letters,* where there are no letters to (or from) Noxon (unless we count Lowry's May 1947 letter to Fletcher Markle), and where Harvey Breit in his Introduction speaks only of New York agent Harold Matson and editor Albert Erskine as (besides Margerie) Lowry's chief aids to survival—we have a palpable Noxon, actively engaged in Lowry's personal and creative welfare. If these letters demythologize, or remythologize, Lowry, they do so too with respect to Noxon.

With their dramatization of Noxon's role in Lowry's writing career, the letters also offer considerable surprise—really a significant revision of the existing biographical record and a striking alteration of the legend—in revealing to us for the first time something of Lowry's method of actually solving problems he encountered in rewriting *Under the Volcano* once and for all. That Lowry in 1940-44 managed on his own to find sufficient inner and outer equilibrium to offer to the world one of the great novels of the century, but then foundered when no agent or editor was on hand to sympathetically carry him forward to further achievement after it appeared in 1947, is an interpretation implicit or explicit in much writing about Lowry. Though it is true that Lowry would have benefited from more sensible collaboration with editors or other readers in those later years, his correspondence with Noxon makes clear how incorrect it is to regard him as having burst in 1940-44 beyond the limited artistic range of the earlier (1936-40) drafts of the novel with help only from Margerie. Gerald Noxon also was periodically on hand, though of course to a much lesser extent than Margerie, to provide stimulation and encouragement, as well as a supportive, empathetic reader's editorial eye.

But Lowry's relationship with Noxon as reader/editor went further yet. As Lowry's "Dear Brother" salutation in one early letter might imply, Noxon was opportunely on hand in 1940 also as one in a series of answers to Lowry's searches for lost brothers, lost fathers, lost grandfathers. Lowry—winking clownishly from the wings (he was, he once boasted, a great "noises off" man)—time and again used his artistic enterprises, both real and proposed, to tease into existence various family-like structures, most obviously in his father/son relationship with Conrad Aiken. Over the years Lowry's writing projects let him place himself in a whole series of family circles, complete with the possibility of family occasion, the trappings of familial trust, forgiveness, loyalty, longing, and solidarity, even the threat of prodigality and the fear of betrayal. Some of the patterns of family-style friendship evident elsewhere—in the beckoning of the rhetoric in letters to Clemens ten Holder of Germany, Frank Taylor of the MGM studios in Hollywood, Hal Matson or Albert Erskine of New York, for example—are repeated in Lowry's correspondence with Noxon. But with Noxon, more consistently than with anyone else— unless we include Lowry's still-unpublished entreaties to Margerie in August and September of 1939, to come and live with him and help him —Lowry's overtures were warmly returned over a long period. In his interaction with Noxon, Lowry found an unusual measure of personal, practical, and intellectual fulfillment, without the tension and conflict, the love/hate, that marked stages of his relationship with Aiken. Mutually felt artistic promptings and personal affection gave to both Lowry and Noxon, as well as to Margerie, a strengthening of the spirit, a sense of emotional and literary survival and well-being, especially in the first half of the 1940s when all three were writing a great deal but publishing almost nothing.*

Lowry desperately needed an editor and a brother in 1940, and the letters in this collection attest to Noxon's energy and purpose in fashioning himself as the willing recipient of the roles Lowry offered him. In 1940

---

*Margerie Lowry's first two novels, *The Last Twist of the Knife* and *The Shapes That Creep,* did not appear until 1946; her third, *Horse in the Sky,* appeared in 1947. Although Noxon had several novels—including *Teresina Maria* (published in 1986 by *The Malcolm Lowry Review*), set in the Italy of Mussolini's regime and begun in 1931-32 in Rome—and a great deal of poetry underway in the 1940s, and wrote many scripts for successful radio broadcast, he did not publish anything during that decade until 1948, when an excerpt from his long poem, "Branches of the Night," appeared in *Canadian Poetry Magazine.*

Noxon became Lowry's connection with the world beyond the wilderness. During the process of Lowry's transforming *Under the Volcano* into its final form, Noxon was willing to become not only Lowry's "brother" but also his "White Man," his "Man from the East." So when the Lowrys finally travelled east to the Toronto area for their long visit beginning in the summer of 1944 and continuing through the "interminable golden bittersweet awful beautiful Eastern autumn" (Lowry, p. 47) to the middle of winter, their acceptance of Noxon's standing invitation to visit was doubly significant: they were going in search of serious last-minute help with *Under the Volcano,* and they were going to visit "family" to get that help. Once they were more or less settled at the Noxons', Lowry would scribble with pleasure and relief in the margins of his manuscript reminders and instructions such as these: "Take to Geralds chap. VI, VII & VIII," "Better get Gerald to read *Lost Weekend,*" "Need Gerald or Margie's help."

Noxon's deftness at skillfully combining the unofficial roles of devoted and jocund family member and literary editor give these letters—often brimming with high spirits and fond affections—an easeful tone missing in much other Lowry correspondence. Surprise and pleasure alike come in our catching Lowry—"vile hermit" that he could be—engaged so fully and so exuberantly, and for so many years, in the simple rituals of a pretty ordinary friendship, a lively friendship not dominated by worries regarding business arrangements, a relaxed friendship more or less free of the parades of desperate pleas or promises marking his later epistolary associations. Here are breezy and buoyant letters celebrating hikes and boat-rides and picnics around the Dollarton shack during the war years, letters not only presenting (sometimes irreverently, as in Lowry's October 1942 comments, where "R.B." must be William Empson, who had been a student of I. A. Richards at Cambridge) favourite topics in literature or film but also describing the favourite chairs and pet cats of the Lowry household, the activities of a Dollarton neighbour whom Noxon had met, the special pleasures of baked oysters, or, in Ontario, the exploits of daredevils like Captain Matthew Webb and Bobby Leach, who had years before gone over the falls at Niagara. Here serious expressions of thought and desire, or frivolous descriptions of the trivialities and routines of daily living, presented amidst a carnival of sometimes dashing, sometimes comical, sometimes solemn embraces, shock us because so often in the *Selected Letters* we observe Lowry desperately clinging to what sometimes seem like fragments of imagined friendships. Here we feel the impact on Lowry of Noxon's visits to "the hideout in Dollarton, which is," as Noxon described it to Aiken, "very beautiful and grand, although almighty primitive" (Noxon, 1945), visits vividly and fondly recalled by Lowry, visits affecting the tone of his life, the texture of his and Margerie's small-talk. On a particularly beautiful day the Lowrys would say to each other, "It's a pity Gerald couldn't be here to see this." Or they might say, "This is rather like that day Gerald was here." As Lowry said to Noxon during that edenic period which ended with the fire in 1944: "Time, when at all, is measured here thus. This is A. D. 2, two years after the advent of the Man From the East!" Noxon's visits verified and amplified for the Lowrys the rightness and wholeness of their world, of the metaphors by which they described their world, where they lived and wrote and played, childlike, as though in a fantastic wonderland.

The roles that Gerald Noxon took over in 1940 were in some ways prepared for him also by Conrad Aiken. Behind the letters in this collection hovers the presence of the American poet and novelist (whom the Lowrys and the Noxons, in a partying mood one day in Ontario in 1944, actually telephoned, though with comically frustrating results when Lowry tried in vain to make himself understood by Aiken; "your telephone voice my lad leaves something to be desired" [Aiken, p. 260], Aiken chided Lowry later). For Lowry, his 1940s relationship with Noxon provided a replacement for his long apprenticeship relationship with Aiken. And his 1940s correspondence with Noxon provided a replacement for his recent exchange of many letters with Aiken, notably those written from the fall of 1939—shortly after he was taken (in late July) by his father's legal representative, the attorney Benjamin Parks, from Los Angeles to Vancouver, where he was joined (in late September) by Margerie—to the summer of 1940. Lowry and Aiken hastily sent twenty or more letters back and forth between Vancouver and Cape Cod in those months alone, with Lowry's centring hopefully on ingenious ways by which Aiken might convince Lowry's quite well-to-do father in Liverpool to once again place him, desperate and helpless as he claimed to be, in Aiken's care, where he might get support to finish the poems and novels he had underway. Lowry wanted Aiken to emphasize to his father that in the west-coast Canadian city he was unreasonably remote from his mentor, that he felt "desperately unhappy, absolutely alone and without friends in an abominable climate," that he was in Canada "among strangers" who did not understand him. He reminded Aiken that however stormy their relationship might have become over the years—most recently in 1937 during Aiken's visit to Lowry and his first wife, Jan Gabrial, in Cuernavaca, Mexico—Aiken still had a kind of moral obligation to him as family member: "you know as well as I that you are far more my father than my own father . . . " (Lowry, pp. 21-23).

Though Aiken was wary of re-establishing personal arrangements which would be too confining, too potentially suffocating or explosively destructive for him, for Lowry, or for them both, he tried to bring Lowry closer to Cape Cod, tried to have him settled at least in Toronto or Montreal. He must have remembered with fondness the invigorating visits which began when his "young genius" sailed from England to the United States in July 1929 to meet him, "to be taught how to write novels." But he must also have felt how complicated their life together had steadily grown. At first, back in 1929, Aiken had thought of "young Lowry" simply as a "nice chap, but incredibly dirty and sloppy and helpless. Writes exceedingly well, and undoubtedly should do something. Very companionable, too . . . " (Aiken, pp. 153-55). However, after several years of weekends and holidays together, while Lowry went through his studies at Cambridge and wrote his first novel, *Ultramarine,* years during which Aiken and his second wife Clarissa Lorenz were living in Rye, there developed stresses and strains in his and Lowry's friendship. These found a focus when Lowry sailed with the Aikens to Spain for a vacation in 1933 (while the recently-married Gerald and Betty Noxon sublet the Aikens' house in Rye). In Spain Lowry was encouraged by Aiken to take up with the American, Jan Gabrial; but her presence, and absences, now complicated not only Lowry's life but also his relationship with Aiken. Lowry married her in Paris in January 1934. He had been drinking for a long time by then, and Jan's company, as well as her frequent departures, did little to slow down his self-destructive bias during the 1930s. In 1939-40 Aiken's memories of seeing Lowry in New York in 1936 (where Lowry had followed Jan from Europe in late 1934) and in Mexico in 1937 (where Aiken, while divorcing Clarissa Lorenz and marrying Mary Hoover, visited Lowry), must have made him shudder at the thought of a full-blown reunion with Lowry. And Aiken's knowledge, when Lowry described his plight in Vancouver, of some of Lowry's other domiciles of the 30s—the Psychiatric Wing of Bellevue Hospital in New York in 1935, a Fascist prison in Mexico in 1937—must have made him squirm with as much fear as sympathy. Whatever the combination of eagerness and trepidation Aiken felt about the prospect of reuniting with his "young Englishman" (Aiken, p. 153), his considerable effort to find a way of bringing Lowry closer to Cape Cod failed.

But if Aiken was unable in 1939-40 to convince Lowry's father that he should revive Aiken's role in a practical way as Lowry's literary intimate, Aiken was able at least to revive the friendship between Lowry and Noxon by announcing to each the news of the other having moved to Canada, and by supplying them with mailing addresses. In Aiken's eyes (as he made clear in letters to Malcolm Cowley and to John Gould

Fletcher) Lowry and Noxon were artistic kin whom he saw as belonging to a group of Cambridge graduates who were his admirers: "good fellows, and gifted, and I like them immensely" (Aiken, p. 275; see also p. 268).

Gerald Noxon met Conrad Aiken in the summer of 1930, when Lowry introduced them to each other in Rye. Noxon had seen Aiken at literary parties in London in the mid-1920s, knew his work, and was even related to Aiken's first wife, Jessie McDonald, a Canadian like himself; but he never had had a chance to get to know Aiken. After that 1930 meeting he and Aiken became good friends. In the early 1930s Noxon published some of Aiken's work in *Experiment,* and later in the decade, shortly before they both returned to North America, he tried to help Aiken find film-work in London. He kept a tiny cottage near Rye from about 1934 to 1940, and in the late 1940s settled near Aiken on Cape Cod. Among the finest radio dramas Noxon ever wrote were adaptations of stories by Aiken. At intervals all along, of course, Noxon and Aiken (whom Noxon has described as both Lowry's "father confessor" and a "great Freudian" always attempting to analyze "Malc") kept each other abreast of the usually turbulent goings-on in Lowry's life.

In any case, when Lowry from the fall of 1939 to the summer of 1940 complained lustily to Aiken about his plight in Canada, Aiken must have been pleased and relieved when, in the summer of 1940, Noxon sailed from England to Canada to join his wife and son, Nicolas, who were both by then with Noxon's relatives near Toronto. The Noxons' three-year-old boy had actually sailed from England to North America in the care of Aiken and his third wife, Mary Hoover, in late September 1939 just after war had broken out. Noxon's wife, Betty Lane, a painter from the Washington area whom Noxon had met in Paris and married in London in 1933, had followed shortly after, and had with Nicolas temporarily settled with Noxon's relatives.

Noxon's coming to Canada answered Lowry's desperate need for a literary "brother" perfectly, especially at the dispiriting time in 1940-41 when the "old" (1940) version of *Under the Volcano* had stopped making futile rounds of New York publishers. In the late summer of 1940 Noxon wrote his first letter to Lowry. From 1941 to 1943, while he was on research and writing assignments in western Canada, Noxon visited the Lowrys at Dollarton at least once a year, staying sometimes for several days in their cabin at Dollarton. There he read Lowry's, as well as Margerie's and his own, work in progress, provided them, as they provided him, with shrewd and informed criticism, and especially concentrated with them, as in a small writers' guild, on Lowry's rewriting of *Under the Volcano.*

Even though the letters published here reveal few of the details of Noxon's direct influence on the content of Lowry's work, they do establish that there was such influence. In recent conversations Noxon himself has shed some light on the measure of his counselling. For example, of just the opening of *Under the Volcano* he has said: "We re-wrote the first paragraph of that book at least twenty times. . . . It's like a shot from space. . . . That was a very definite aim of his—to achieve a kind of world view and lead us into this thing knowing where we are—and I approved of that very much—I liked the way he did it in the end and I think that this first scene with Vigil and Laruelle is a tremendous opening—it really makes me feel comfortable." What the letters do convey, especially through Lowry's repeated testimony, is a strong sense of the general design and quality and impact of Noxon's guidance. They show him expertly taking up a position like the one he had occupied at Cambridge University a decade before, as Lowry's editor ("my first editor," as Lowry now called him). For example, they reveal that from the beginning of his first appearance in British Columbia, he responded positively to Lowry's insistence that he listen to his work and help in assessing it. "I look to you very earnestly for criticism," Lowry stated right after that meeting, during which he read at great length to Noxon, "which was given and has already been most useful." After Noxon's Dollarton visit in the summer of 1942, Lowry briskly reported that he had "wrought 100% improvements thanks to you, in the early pachydermatous prose of the *Volcano*." In 1943 Lowry wrote that he hoped to "inflict" his manuscript on Noxon again as it "smoulder[ed] to a finish in reverse, first chapter last."

Even after he jubilantly announced to Noxon in an April 15, 1946 telegram, "VOLCANO ACCEPTED LONDON NEW YORK," Lowry pleaded with him to carry on as his editorial reader. When the New York publisher informed him of possible changes to the manuscript, Lowry wrote to Noxon: "have you any suggestions—you know how I value your opinion." Later: "I would have been better off for your advice re possible cuts etc." When the London publisher requested a preface and a "blurb," he asked Noxon: "Can you help? I am in a considerable stew about what to say. . . . I await your advice." Lowry summed up Noxon's role in the creation of *Under the Volcano* when he thanked him for his "own part in and encouragement re the book. All your suggestions turned out right, and the parts you sat on . . . and which I rewrote with Margie's and your help until they got your O. K. have become the strongest."

Gerald Noxon (b. 1910) had always worked easily with strong creative personalities: Jacob Bronowski, William Empson, and other fellow edi-

tors involved with the little magazine, *Experiment;* film-makers and artists such as John Grierson, Stuart Legg, Humphrey Jennings, Basil
Wright, and Len Lye; various radio producers in England, Canada, and
the United States; writers such as Conrad Aiken and, of course, Lowry.
Though not all of Noxon's collaborations ran smoothly (for example,
Grierson not only hired but also fired him at least three times), he could
work admirably on a co-operative basis. He had the capacity not only for
identifying genius, but also for expressing friendship by actively sup-
porting it, being attendant upon it, whether as editor, publisher, critic,
promoter, or as adapter of literary texts.

With Lowry, Noxon responded readily, as early as 1930 in England,
to what he thought of as the "true" Lowry, a spontaneously witty and
friendly, if shy, individual, a man of great spiritual and emotional depth
and sensitivity whom he could discern beneath the swaggering
sailor/poet known in bars around Cambridge, an artist "full of laughter
and joy, conscious, though never confident, of his talent and ability"
(Noxon, 1964). He very much liked this Lowry, from whom he saw
emanating for the first time, during their few days together in Rye in the
summer of 1930, not just a sense of personal malady but also a dazzling
talent for friendship: "Malcolm proved himself a fascinating companion.
The brilliance of his mind, his extraordinary memory, the amazing range
of depth of his knowledge, his fund of really funny stories in which the
jokes were most often at his own expense, all astonished and captivated
me as did the warmth and friendliness of his nature, which was revealed
to me in its true condition for the first time" (Noxon, 1964). In January
1946 Noxon expressed even stronger sentiments directly to Lowry.
"[R]emember," he said in a burst of emotion, in the midst of a confusing
period of several months when he knew nothing precise of Lowry's
plans, his whereabouts, or the disposition of his manuscript of *Under the
Volcano,* "you have been one of the few artists that I have admired, one
of the very few men that I have trusted and one of the few writers that I
have read, feeling that I was in the presence of genius."

Noxon's statements of affection should not suggest that he was blind
to Lowry's shortcomings: to his awkward impositions, his fits, his
depressions. Noxon—tolerant, indulgent—simply was able to accept
Lowry as an unusually burdensome friend, "a difficult person to deal
with, very, very difficult"; but Noxon has said recently that he probably
"got along with him as well as anybody did. And that was Margerie's
impression too." To be sure, Noxon's eulogistic letter of January 1946
was written after a period of particular hardship and strain in the relationship some months before. When the Lowrys had come to live near, and
for long weeks with, the Noxons in Ontario in 1944-45 after the fire at

Dollarton, Lowry had behaved badly as a guest. True, he had felt the soothing impact of the pastoral world surrounding the Noxons in the "Ontario backwoods" around Oakville and Niagara-on-the-Lake, a charming village which he described to Aiken as "something to see: really beautiful" (Lowry, p. 48). But during that long visit he had been—as he confided to Aiken—"in shocking bad form and worse company. . . . How the Noxons bore with me—if they really did—I don't know. Actually the business of the fire seemed to drive us slightly cuckoo. Its traumatic effect alone was shattering. We had to live through the bloody fire all over again every night. I would wake to find Margie screaming or she would wake to find me yelling and gnashing my teeth" (Lowry, p. 48). Noxon, too, wrote Aiken. When the fire chased them "out of the garden," the Lowrys were left "in a state which had to be seen to be understood," he said. " When they got to our place they were in a monstrous turmoil and re-lived the whole fire incident every single night for weeks. . . . Anyway we eventually got Malc to work on finishing the *Volcano* and he immediately showed great improvement" (Noxon, 1945). The Lowrys' affairs, Noxon said to Aiken once their visit with the Noxons in Ontario had ended, "have given me a good deal of worry in the past eight months. One does what one can for them but there is a point beyond which no one can help and one can discover that point only by trial and error" (Noxon, 1945).

For his part, then, even with a cantankerous Lowry on his hands, Noxon—making room for Lowry as artist and as friend—simply extended generous hospitality, however trying the immediate circumstances. He, like Margerie, deliberately sustained Lowry with gestures of encouragement and support, always assuring the insecure Lowry of his worthiness, his goodness, his greatness, his rightness. Noxon was steadfastly determined to join the performance, the dance with which Lowry flamboyantly, in fits and starts, kept his own spirit whirling and alive. Noxon was determined, both as audience and fellow performer, and with encouragement from the Lowrys, to help in keeping the performance (notwithstanding its "routine looniness," to use Margerie's term) from faltering—at the very least until *Under the Volcano* was safely in bookstores.

When his task of getting Lowry to complete the manuscript was finished, Noxon's lengthy report to Aiken brimmed with details of Lowry's achievement: "I don't know how well you are acquainted with his book—*Under the Volcano*—or how much he may have written you about it, but he has tried, with a great deal of success in my opinion, to put into it all the things which have happened to him since he was born and as a shape he has chosen the triple world of the *Divine Comedy*. Dante's conception has in fact become Malc's overpowering obsession and every single thing has to be worked into it somehow or other. . . . It is very beautiful and also very frightening, packed with layer upon layer of meaning, so that as you re-read you uncover more and more. . . . Malc's ability as a writer has developed tremendously and if he can only maintain his very precarious balance mentally, he will go on turning out great things" (Noxon, 1945).

Malcolm Lowry and Gerald Noxon first met each other in the fall of 1929 when Lowry went up to Cambridge—to St. Catharine's College— and began a search for literary contacts. One of the people whom he sought out was Noxon, publishing editor of *Experiment* and something of a poet. Though born a year later than Lowry, Noxon was Lowry's senior by one year at Cambridge. Their meeting in Noxon's rooms in Trinity College led immediately to the publication of Lowry's short story, "Port Swettenham," in the February 1930 (number 5) issue of *Experiment*.

But Lowry's meeting with Noxon in 1929 benefited Lowry even more, for Noxon was connected also with other great loves of Lowry's: jazz (Noxon's collection of New Orleans jazz records was impressive) and, above all, film. Noxon, zealous in introducing serious film to England, was president and chief organizer of one of England's first major film societies, the Cambridge Film Guild, which he helped found in 1929. He was full-time film-review editor and frequent film reviewer for the weekly paper, *Granta,* and he was contributor of learned treatises and more informal reports on film (as well as the other arts, such as photography and painting) to *The Cambridge Review* and even *transition* in France. He had ties with the film journal, *Close Up,* published by Bryher from 1927 to 1933 on the continent, with the London Film Society, founded in 1925, and with the Shaftesbury Avenue Pavilion Cinema (featured later in Lowry's fiction) in London, which was widely known for its international program from 1928 to 1930. At university, Noxon was friends with Jennings and Wright. With Stuart Legg he co-directed a 1931 documentary entitled *Cambridge.* From 1926 to 1928, in the two years between public school at Stowe and university, Noxon had spent almost all his time in Paris, where he had kept up with avant-garde and other developments in Russian and west-European film as much as in literature. Further, at social gatherings in Paris and in London in the 1920s he had seen not only Eliot and Joyce and Wyndham Lewis, as well as Aiken, but also the film-makers Eisenstein and Pudovkin, Man Ray and Cavalcanti. So at Cambridge he and Lowry talked not only about writers and writing, but also about contemporary film directors from France and Russia, as well as from America. And they talked about the Expressionist and other films Lowry had seen in Germany when he had studied in Bonn in 1928.

It is interesting to note, here, that Noxon's personal identification with his native Canada was strong, and in Lowry's 1929-31 associations with Noxon-as-Canadian we see prefigurations of Lowry's later responses to Canada. Noxon, whose ancestors had moved to Canada with the United Empire Loyalists, whose birthplace was Toronto (even though his schooling after World War I was centred in continental Europe and England), and whose own father in the 1920s and 1930s acted in London not not only as Agent-General for Ontario but also, for practical purposes, as High Commissioner for Canada, was from an early age sensitive to the potential for Canada's cultural development, and spoke about it with Lowry. In 1930 in Cambridge he published some of his views in *Films and the State,* a booklet demonstrating the educational prospects for government-supported cinema in Canada (a proposal appreciatively read upon its appearance by Canadian Prime Minister Mackenzie King, and one which might have had some effect on King's determination to create the National Film Board of Canada, under John Grierson, in 1939). In the early 1940s in Canada some of his first radio-drama series (to which the Lowrys would listen) unabashedly tried to lead audiences to appreciate the greatness in Canada's past, present, and future. In 1944-45, when the Lowrys were living with the Noxons in Niagara-on-the-Lake, once the capital of Upper Canada, Noxon was an active member of a historical society dedicated to preserving and restoring the town's earlier beauty.

Lowry was undoubtedly attracted by Noxon's good-natured presence in England as an enterprising and efficient colonial visitor, a kind of outsider, from a land known to Lowry for its rain forests and glacial lakes and snow-capped, pine-clad mountains—from a land connected with images like those Noxon would regularly display at Cambridge in the form of advertisements his father's London office sent to *Experiment.* Time and again full-page sketches with captions beckoning readers to a land of the "Great Outdoors," with its "Slopes of the Sunny Pacific," its "Wonderful Rockies and Pacific Coast," a land where "sunny days and cool nights strengthen and refresh you," found a place among the literary pages of that little magazine. A decade later, in Canada, Lowry's own profusion of images in his letters to Noxon seem to ecstatically echo some of those very descriptions. He seemed to be trying to put on, to outdo, those travel notices with his own dancing references to the rugged beauty surrounding him at Dollarton, with sharply imagistic statements about his role in a wilderness pageant, a role which he appropriated as much in mythic as in actual terms.

In the early 1930s, after he graduated from Cambridge in 1931, Noxon saw Lowry again only a few times, mainly in London, not at all on the continent—though chance might just as easily have brought them together there, for Noxon was often in Paris. (In a 1932 letter to Aiken, Lowry implies that he has just had some contact with Noxon.) In 1931-32 Noxon put his knowledge of French and Italian to work as a translator and editor of the monthly film review of the International Institute of Educational Cinematography in Rome. Disgusted at Mussolini's use of the Institute as a political tool, he left in frustration, though not without having steeped himself in experiences which found their way into his political satire, *Teresina Maria*. Noting that it had developed politically respectable links with the League of Nations, Noxon charged that the Institute "fails to advance the truly international purposes of the cinema"; its intention, he said, "is not educational but political. It is not an international institute in any sense: it merely exploits internationalism for its own national propaganda purposes" (Noxon, 1934). Noxon returned to England and, from 1932 to 1940, worked in a variety of positions in London involving either film or radio production or both, whether for commercial interests (including his own company, Spectator Short Films), for the BBC, or for John Grierson's documentary film units. When he moved to Canada in 1940 to work at least briefly for the National Film Board of Canada, he continued his 1930s associations not only with John Grierson but also with Stuart Legg, who had become Grierson's right-hand man at the Board.

So it was with a background of considerable contact with some of the most exciting artistic developments of the time that Noxon settled in Canada to work on film and, beginning in 1941 with the Canadian Broadcasting Corporation, on radio. It was a cosmopolitan Noxon upon whom, after an almost ten-year hiatus, Lowry burst, offering in his first letter a happily gibing formality, a deft and endearing bridging of the years, "In reply to yours of July, 1930 . . . ." Lowry's grinning nudges of boyish charm, so effervescently explicit in all the pleasure and relief and camaraderie directly expressed in the first few letters reproduced here, affect the tone of the entire collection. Lowry luxuriated in warmly and wittily and playfully beckoning Noxon to take a place in the romance of his fresh new life in the Canadian wilderness, and—as though referring to the impossible and hilarious pieces of a charade, or to undergraduate escapades, exploits, pranks—lightly offered him vivid descriptions of a hellish past, of his "vexing Christmas" in Mexico, for example, "cooling my heels in a fascist dungeon." In such letters we might actually be hard-pressed to determine just what part of Lowry's Mexico of 1936-38 was hell, what part send-up.

From the beginning of the correspondence, then, with the friendly cajoling of Lowry's opening letters, Noxon drew on his own personal and artistic resources, on his generous, humane idealism, on his ability to function harmoniously as critic with artists who were his close friends, on his tendency to lend support to a "Better Thing," however it might be expressed. He repeatedly urged the Lowrys to come east to take jobs there, invited them to come to visit at the large house at Oakville where the Noxons settled in 1943, sent them $200 to make the train journey eastward after their shack burned down in 1944, and helped them to find a place in Niagara-on-the-Lake when the Noxons moved to the "Kirby House" there later that year; such were among the kindnesses that Noxon steadfastly showed the Lowrys in those years.

Noxon's support was invaluable, finally, in helping Lowry in 1945 take decisive action regarding *Under the Volcano*—even though Lowry left Noxon in the dark for some time in this respect. In September 1945, with Noxon's praise of Lowry's manuscript as "a wonderful book, a really important piece of writing that will stand the test of time" (Noxon, 1945) ringing in his ears, Conrad Aiken wrote one of his relatively infrequent letters of the 1940s to Lowry. He echoed Noxon's primary concern, indeed, what Noxon has seen as his greatest contribution to *Under the Volcano,* that of getting Lowry to overcome his fear of finishing his masterpiece, to see that the manuscript should be let go: "Gerald wrote me at great length in praise of your book—why not let it come out, my dear fellow? cut the umbilical cord? I'd love to see it" (Aiken, pp. 263-64). What Aiken and Noxon did not know was that a few months earlier Lowry had done just that. After having returned to Dollarton from Ontario in February 1945, Margerie had—despite her and Lowry's ordeal of having to build a new cabin alongside unwanted neighbours who now occupied their burnt-out site, and despite a serious injury to her foot—typed a clean copy. (Lowry had given another copy of the fourth and final draft to the Noxons for Christmas 1944, with the inscription, "in sincere gratitude and friendship . . . with love from Malc.") And in June 1945, without informing either Noxon or Aiken that he had, indeed, cut the umbilical cord, Lowry had finally managed to send off the freshly typed copy to his agent, Harold Matson.

In the covering letter he sent along with the manuscript, Lowry spoke to Matson with surprising timidity and doubt about his work, about imposing "the new *Under the Volcano*" (Lowry, p. 45) on Matson, after the earlier version had been so roundly rejected by New York publishers a little more than four years before. He chose instead to lavish praise on the novels and poems which his "first editor" had underway: "A great friend of mine who was at college with me—a well-known radioman in

Canada, ex-editor of *Experiment,* etc., . . . —has written . . . a very interesting and moving novel centred in pre-war Italy entitled *Teresina
Maria:* I told him he could not do better than send it to you and I hope he
has done so and if so that it will meet with your approval. . . . [H]e is also
an excellent poet and has lots of things boiling, including two other
novels and many short stories. I think he would be a very good venture if
he could get re-started in the literary field, which he was away from to
some extent while concerned in radio, movies, etc., not to say the
English blitz. His name is Gerald Noxon—very familiar here, as I say,
on the air" (Lowry, pp. 46-47). Matson, to whom Noxon had submitted
his novel, assured Lowry that both *Under the Volcano* and *Teresina
Maria* were being read.

Lowry's desire to help Noxon expand his activities to the "literary"
field brings to mind again the considerable interest and activity not only
of Noxon but also of Lowry in several other artistic areas; indeed, during
the period of the present correspondence a surprising amount of work in
radio and film ran alongside even the Lowrys' literary efforts. Most
notably with respect to film, the Lowrys in 1949-50 wrote their outstand-
ing 455-page filmscript, a meta-cinematic adaptation of F. Scott
Fitzgerald's novel, *Tender Is the Night.* Noxon's main film contribution
occurred in late 1940, when he directed the first French-language film in
the *Canada Carries On* series, *Un du 22ième,* a semi-documentary,
semi-dramatic short designed to inspire French-Canadian participation in
the war effort. Most of Lowry's and Noxon's dreams about film-making
were unfulfilled. For example, in Noxon's first letter to Lowry, in
Lowry's last letter to Noxon, and in letters in between, each saw possibilities of collaborating with the other in film-writing ventures, none of
which materialized. (In 1941 even Aiken tried—though unsuccess-
fully—to use his influence with Stuart Legg to get Lowry a job with the
National Film Board of Canada.)

In radio, Noxon's success was pronounced. During what is often
called "the golden age" of Canadian radio-drama, from 1944 to 1955,
he developed one of Canada's finest reputations as radio dramatist. It
was, as we have noted, already in 1941-44 in Canada that he began to
turn his 1930s BBC radio experience into profit with two thirteen-week
dramatic series, *They Fly for Freedom* and *Our Canada* (or *Joe,* as the
Lowrys preferred to call it, after its main character), and a 33-week *News
from Europe* series. And already in those years he began to encourage the
Lowrys to consider radio work, too. Andrew Allan in 1940-43 had been
making a name for himself as producer of radio drama at the CBC's Vancouver studios, and the Lowrys did at least go to see him, though without
taking on any radio work just then. In his memoirs he recalls "Lowry

and his pretty blonde wife [coming] to my office to see if there was any radio writing to be done" (Allan, p. 126). It was during that period in Vancouver, too, that Fletcher Markle (radio producer in 1947 for Noxon's version of *Under the Volcano*) wrote some of his early plays, which Allan produced, and which contributed to making Vancouver a vigorous centre for Canadian radio drama (with poets Earle Birney and Dorothy Livesay, both of whom became friends of the Lowrys in the late 1940s, among the key participants).

It was when Allan was promoted to his position as head of radio drama at the CBC in Toronto in 1943, and in January 1944 started the *Stage* series which ran successfully into the era of television, to 1955, that Noxon began to take his own writing for radio more seriously than before. Three of the first dozen or so weekly dramas of *Stage 44* were by Noxon (another four by Markle, who, like Allan, had moved from Vancouver to Toronto). During 1944-45, the season of *Stage 45*, when the Lowrys were staying with the Noxons, Noxon wrote another five plays for Allan's show, and made some contacts so the Lowrys could get involved in Toronto-based radio drama too. So Margerie, with help from her husband, wrote several dramatic scripts—*Maria Chapdelaine, Grey Owl, Sunshine Sketches of a Little Town*—which were produced by the CBC, though in the last case in a form quite altered from the Lowrys' original. In 1946 Lowry gleefully recalled in a letter to Jonathan Cape, "A year or so ago my wife and I were hitting the high places in radio," and he asked if Cape could help get into the BBC a proposed *Moby Dick* script, which Noxon had encouraged him to write and which he in 1945 had planned to submit to the CBC in thirteen weekly installments; the script was, he said, "of a character to completely revolutionize radio" (Lowry, p. 130).

In 1948 Noxon introduced Andrew Allan to Conrad Aiken. The meeting, on Cape Cod, led to the production of one of the finest radio plays broadcast in Canada in the 1940s and 1950s, Noxon's adaptation of Aiken's "Mr. Arcularis" (CBC, 1948). In 1949-50, Noxon's radio versions of three other of Aiken's works were produced by Allan for the CBC: "The Fallen Disciple," "Impulse," and (based on *Conversation*) "A Thief in the House." In a letter to Seymour Lawrence, editor of *Wake* magazine, Lowry praised the "hair-raising and first-rate radio dramas" (Lowry, p. 272) Noxon had made out of their old friend's stories. By 1950 nineteen of Noxon's plays had been produced on Andrew Allan's annual *Stage* program.

Noxon's growing success in radio eventually removed him from Lowry's world, and Lowry (as he said in a "begging" letter to his brother, Stuart, in 1950) again had "no friends in Canada save three fishermen in like case, a cat, five wild ducks, two seagulls, and, of course, a wolf" (Lowry, p. 221). In effect, Noxon had been losing touch with Lowry since 1947, when the production of his radio version of *Under the Volcano* (on CBS's *Studio One* program produced by Fletcher Markle in New York, a few weeks after Noxon had introduced Markle to Lowry in Ontario) marked a step in the transfer of his activities away from his native country, to the eastern States. By 1951 Noxon had established himself in America, where for years he led a new graduate program in film and radio studies at Boston University. Having in 1940 appeared in Canada at just the moment to be of service to Lowry, Noxon, in moving to where he might develop a career more profitably than was possible for him just then in Canada, unintentionally abandoned what was again to become a foundering Lowry.

During the last decade of his life, when Lowry was trying desperately to maintain relations with publishers in New York, trying to convince them of his worth by issuing proclamations outlining the work he had underway, he wrote with some melancholy and nostalgia to Noxon: "we only wish to God we were lucky enough to have your counsel at the moment in regard to Work in Progress." Lowry seemed to recognize that without help such as Noxon's his contracts with publishers were little more than imaginary; yet, in his last letter to Noxon, he did cheerfully hint at maybe being able to repay the $200 Noxon had lent him in 1944. "[We have] never ceased to think of you," Lowry said in 1952, recalling Noxon's visits of a decade before, "always expect and look for your step on the rural stair, from time to time retrace the walks and the talks of a decade ago. Nothing is lost, nothing forgotten . . . ."

Though Noxon managed to publish only a little of his own work during the 1940s, Lowry still regarded him as a kindred spirit who managed to keep alive "the creative artist within." He saw Noxon as a writer capable, too, of coping practically with the pressures of routines in the day-to-day world, including the regularly imposed deadlines of weekly radio programs: "certainly not easy when a creative artist," Lowry said to Noxon, "and the mode of grappling not sufficiently off centre to art not to tempt you away from creating altogether; I can't think of a harder problem . . . ." Lowry's support of Noxon as writer, and his sympathetic expression of anguish in the 1950s, when it was Noxon's and not just his own life that was in turmoil, are demonstrations of his capacity to respond in kind to Noxon's many forms of supportiveness. At the end of the correspondence published here Lowry had the chance to offer one of the most emotional outbursts among the gestures of personal support either man openly expressed in the correspondence. Noxon's marriage had broken apart, and when he expressed his despair at his situation Lowry blurted out heart-felt lament and mourning: "Oh Jesus, . . . my poor old Gerald. . . . [I]t seems incomprehensible." With the correspondence having taken such a sombre turn in light of Noxon's plight, Lowry—in one of two final letters made poignant by what we now can see was a mixture of bravado and desperation and hope, gratitude and nostalgia and longing—took the opportunity to make clear his, and Margerie's, feelings toward Noxon, toward the friendship between them and him: "you are undoubtedly one of the best friends and indeed one of the only real friends I have—or we have." These letters are a testimony to Lowry's and Noxon's friendship.

THE TEXT

The correspondence comprises letters—typed originals and carbon copies, as well as holographs—housed in the Lowry collection at the Humanities Research Center, The University of Texas at Austin and, in much smaller number, in the collection of Lowry manuscripts in the Special Collections Division, The University of British Columbia. It includes also telegrams and night letters (items 29, 30, 32, 49, 50, 63, 64, 65, 66, 69, 70, 75) or (as in the case of the crudely handwritten item 32) drafts of these, a birthday card (item 15), a Christmas card (item 59), postcards (items 11, 18, 42, 47, 58, 61, 67, 77), a list of instructions in Margerie Lowry's hand concerning daily household chores (item 37), and (with item 44) an approximation of an illustration originally drawn by Margerie Lowry. Note that item 53 is the verso of item 52; in the original, item 56 stands as an addition to item 55, item 79 to 78.

In the letters, as also in our introductions, square brackets indicate editorial reconstruction, conjecture, or commentary. At the same time, we have silently standardized the titles of manuscripts and published works referred to by the correspondents. We have also standardized the spelling of words in general, but have done so by following the forms most often used by the writers themselves. Of course, where words seem to have been intentionally misspelled—both Lowry and Noxon made errors rarely—they have been reproduced as in the original.

There are several gaps in the correspondence. In some cases, of course, visits replaced correspondence. But such letters from Noxon as must have preceded items 4, 12, 18, 19, and 78 are missing.

We have taken the dates given on most of the letters from the manuscripts, wherever possible. In the case of postcards, postmarks have helped us determine dates. Square brackets indicate our own reconstruction of dates, or place of origin of the message.

SOURCES AND EDITIONS USED

In our introductions, nearly all of the quotations not annotated are from the letters published here. Three or four such quotations in the main introduction are from recent conversations between Paul Tiessen and Gerald Noxon; another, in the brief introduction preceding letters 67-76, is from a recent conversation between Paul Tiessen and Fletcher Markle.

Published works quoted in the introductions (and abbreviated as indicated) include:

Aiken, Conrad. *Selected Letters of Conrad Aiken,* edited by Joseph Killorin. New Haven: Yale University Press, 1978 (cited as Aiken, with page reference).

Allan, Andrew. *Andrew Allan: A Self-Portrait.* Toronto: Macmillan of Canada, 1974 (cited as Allan, with page reference).

Lowry, Malcolm. *Selected Letters of Malcolm Lowry,* edited by Harvey Breit and Margerie Bonner Lowry. Philadelphia: J. B. Lippincott, 1965 (cited as Lowry, with page reference).

Noxon, Gerald. "In Connection with Malcolm Lowry," with introduction and notes by Paul Tiessen, *The Malcolm Lowry Review,* 17-18 (Fall 1985-Spring 1986): 10-24, transcribed for publication from a 1961 taped radio reminiscence; reprinted in *"On Malcolm Lowry" and Other Writings by Gerald Noxon,* edited by Miguel Mota and Paul Tiessen. Waterloo, Ontario: The Malcolm Lowry Review, 1987, pp. 11-25 (cited as Noxon, 1961).

———. "Italy's 'International' Institute," *Cinema Quarterly* 3 (1934): 12-14 (cited as Noxon, 1934).

———. "Letter to Conrad Aiken [March 1945]," in *"On Malcolm Lowry" and Other Writings by Gerald Noxon,* pp. 26-31 (cited as Noxon, 1945).

———. "Malcolm Lowry: 1930," *Prairie Schooner* 37 (1964): 315-20 (cited as Noxon, 1964).

Though the letters in this collection often in effect modify Douglas Day's *Malcolm Lowry* (New York: Oxford University Press, 1973), it is chiefly to Day that we are indebted for the general biographical information about Lowry in our introductions, as well as in the chronology.

Several of Gerald Noxon's manuscripts which are discussed in the present correspondence have been published recently by *The Malcolm Lowry Review* (Department of English, Wilfrid Laurier University, Waterloo, Ontario). First, Noxon's novel, *Teresina Maria* (248 pp.), with an introduction by Miguel Mota and Paul Tiessen, was published in

1986. In their comments of April 24, 1944, the Lowrys make reference to chapters 1-19 of *Teresina Maria;* readers should note that Noxon renumbered the chapters some time after the Lowrys read them in 1944, and that the chapters cited by the Lowrys are in fact chapters 1-8 (approximately the first half) of the published version.

Furthermore, *"On Malcolm Lowry" and Other Writings by Gerald Noxon,* a collection of essays, letters, poetry, fiction, and radio drama, was published in 1987. It includes (on pp. 151-55) precisely those stanzas (I, IV, VI, XIX, XXX, XXXIV) of "Branches of the Night" which Noxon sent to the Lowrys in 1942, and which they discuss at length in their letter of October 29, 1942. It includes also (on pp. 160-63) stanzas XIV, XV, XLI, and LX of "Branches of the Night," which Noxon introduces to the Lowrys in his letter of August 2, 1947, and (on pp. 111-46) three of the chapters ("Birth," "School," and "Death") of the novel, "Clegg's Wall," which Noxon describes in his June 1, 1945 letter to the Lowrys.

Malcolm Lowry's 35-page "Work in Progress" summary of "The Voyage that Never Ends" (November 1951) was published in *The Malcolm Lowry Review*, 21 (Fall 1987). We mention it in our introduction to Letters 78–80.

PART I

August 1940 to May 1944

LETTERS 1-6

August 1940 to January 1941

In the opening letters Lowry evokes his and Noxon's Cambridge University period with references to their friends and contacts of those years: John Davenport, Julian Trevelyan, Hugh Sykes-Davies, Michael Redgrave, Tom Harrison, and Tom Forman, who were part of the literary scene at Cambridge; Lowry's friend from Oxford, the writer Arthur Calder-Marshall; Noxon's friend, the filmmaker Len Lye.

Four years after Lowry's death, in his 1961 radio broadcast, recently published as "In Connection with Malcolm Lowry" (Noxon, 1961), Noxon also recalled something of life at Cambridge, and noted how busy Lowry had been with the writing and rewriting of *Ultramarine*: "It went through, as did all Malcolm's literary work, great metamorphoses and was produced under conditions that were fairly chaotic. However, either from excerpts from that book or from separate passages which never perhaps appeared finally in *Ultramarine* . . . I think everybody was agreed . . . that here was a writer of talent. Exactly how this talent was going to work itself out it was quite impossible to say at that time, because Malcolm did have certain very grave problems to solve, as well as many problems of a personal nature which I don't intend to go into. But one of his great problems from a literary point of view at that time was—as with most writers who are starting their first serious work—it was to evolve a style, a way of writing which would be reasonably consistent with what he had to say, the subject matter that he wanted to deal with, and the breadth and scope of his understanding." As Lowry's fellow undergraduate at Cambridge Noxon felt—as he was to feel again in Canada in the early 1940s—that Lowry "was suffering from a sort of involuted and overly baroque kind of style which made him very difficult, in some cases, to read. And unnecessarily difficult. . . . I didn't see very much of him and when I did see him it was usually to discuss a specific piece of work or to try to get him to put down on paper things which he had discussed; in other words, the kind of things that most publishers have to do: to try to extract copy from an author for whose work they have considerable regard."

The several days Lowry and Noxon enjoyed together in 1930 in Rye, where Lowry was spending some of his summer holiday with Conrad Aiken and Aiken's (then) wife, Clarissa Lorenz, prefigured the general pleasures of Lowry's and Noxon's 1940s friendship in Canada: "I was staying for several days in the neighbourhood and much of this time Malcolm and I spent together going around from one pub to another, of which there is an incredible number in even so small a place as Rye, and going swimming out off Camber sands. . . . [W]e didn't talk much about books, we talked more about places and about ideas in general—I felt that during those few days I got to know him very much better than I had ever known him up at Cambridge and I became more than ever conscious of the problems which he had to solve as a person, and, also, I gathered some of the reasons for these problems, which were of long standing and arising out of his childhood. . . . [I]t was an extremely revealing and extraordinarily fascinating time as far as I was concerned. And I began to understand the directions in which Malcolm's talent might lead him if he were able to achieve a sufficient degree of stability to become the writer that he so obviously was capable of becoming from the point of view of talent."

After that holiday, Noxon and Lowry actually saw little of each other until they both happened to move to Canada in 1939-40: "our paths lay in quite different directions," Noxon recalled in 1961 of their years after Cambridge. "All through the thirties I had occasional news of him: that he was writing, that he was not writing, that he was . . . in France, in Spain and so forth, travelling, that he was married. . . . [B]ut I did not have any idea of what he was actually doing in the way of writing."

1

Dollarton P. O.
Dollarton, B. C.
August 26, 1940

My very dear old Gerald Noxon, by God!

Throw that highly important letter you are writing straight out of the window and drop me a line instantly.

I heard from Conrad, who seems in marvellous form, that you were in Toronto, where we'd been planning, this summer, to go, incidentally, though we were frustrated. Wonderful news. How are you, man? For heaven's sake tell me quick? I haven't seen a human face it seems in a decade, have snarled at no human beast in a year. And how are John Davenport, Julian Trevelyan, Hugh Sykes, Michael Redgrave? Do you know, and if you do, how are Tom Harrison, Tom Forman, Arthur Calder-Marshall? Who is dead, or imprisoned, or interned and what kind of hope do any of them or us hold out if any of anything?

I came here to Canada from U. S. just before the war, couldn't get back to the States when it broke out, probably, now, can never go back. My MSS etc. were all on the other side of the border, not to say money, and a wife, who has since divorced me. I volunteered, however, to go to England and enlist and was told to stay here, which I did, that is, stay: as for enlisting, I shall probably hear from the Canadian navy circa 1960, just in time to help blockade the Doukhobors. Meantime, I have been and am on, as someone said, the horns of a Domelia. Perhaps you can make matters a bit clearer to me, the Domelia less uncomfortable: the war, that is! I can't hew my way through the sanctifications into any kind of daylight. I do not care, I tell myself at present, to live in a world where everyone cheats, so do not live in it, but rather, like Timon of Athens, on the edge of it: a shack on the sea in a deserted village. Once this was a place where they built ships (Dollar liners): only evidence of this now are the slipways overgrown with meadowsweet and blackberries and the forest. It is a fine wet ruin of a forest full of snakes and snails and terrific trees blasted with hail and fire. We dive from our front porch into a wild sea troughing with whales and seals. We have a boat, now diving at anchor. Everywhere there is a good smell of sea and timber and life and death and crabs.

"We" are Margerie Bonner, the ex movie (child, silent) star and I. We plan to marry in October. If this looks like cradle snatching I ought to point out that the said child film star is now of age. Since November '39 I've written two novels: there is a book of pomes: am hoping Lippincott and Story Press will take the whole bolus of my work—approx. 5 tomes in all, excluding early plagarations, beginning with *Under the Volcano,* a novel about Mexico. (Where I spent a vexing Christmas cooling my heels in a fascist dungeon, expecting to be shot.) So that you see, or if you don't see, I should point out, that with me, in spite of the Timonesque surroundings, it is going well. But one cannot live forever in peace of mind without knowing what is happening to those one loves and respects in the ex-world.

Do you recollect that you are my first editor? Ten years ago we took a Camber train, walked Camber beach: Hugh Sykes was going to be married. We drank much beer, and smoked Balkan (it's like eatin') Sobranie. You told me then about the economic situation in Canada in terms I now comprehend somewhat better. Now, will you please tell me the truth about this bleeding war and what you imagine is going to happen? It may be, if one is really needed in England, I should go there on my own hook: should I? No one can say but myself, who has just discovered it's really very good to be alive. But you can tell me, so far as you are able, what I cannot read, and may not wholly deduce, the truth: the truth, at least, as you see it. So, let's have it, please, unvarnished, and unsurrounded by loud gregarious lies as it must be. For one thing, how long do you think it (the war) is going to go on, at least in its present outward form?

Conrad tells me you may go to the States. I don't think I *can,* but still hope. But I do look forward to some opportunity of seeing you. If you are broke though, or in need of sanctuary, or somewhere to invite the soul where you will be insulated from the current pandemonium in everything but intellect, or all of these things, or none, why not come here? We have about enough money, if all our projects fail, to last till December: I have this *Volcano* book boiling: Margie is on the point of selling a detective novel. We pay $10 a month (!) for our shack: there are lots of other shacks, creaking "live here" in the southwest wind. It would be swell to see you. It is a magnificent place to live, work, or commit suicide. Julian (*Midnight*) Green may make a dark journey here. Count on us, if you need to count: and bear us, you and your wife, to whom all the best, in mind, anyhow.

The baked oysters are calling! *And every night the supper wine;* not forgetting, either, the Balkan (it's like eatin'), Sobranie.

In reply to yours of July, 1930, inst. etc., I am

Very respectfully yours etc.,
Malcolm Lowry

2

Windsor Hotel
Montreal or thereabouts
(It's hard to say)
September 15 [1940]

Dear Malcolm,

I have feelings of the very greatest shame on account of I have not answered your welcome letter earlier. It did not in fact reach me very soon but when it did catch up with me I was with my wife at Mr. Conrad Aiken's new house on Cape Cod. Can I say of Conrad and Mary more than that they are in the very top of form. In the evenings they glisten with gin and in the mornings with sweat because they work so hard getting the place into shape. They are very very anxious indeed to see you both there prontissimo if you can possibly get back into the States.

I am working for the National Film Board of Canada on a sort of independent producer basis and am just about to start on a film about a French Canadian regiment at a place called Valcartier P. Q. I am sorry but I cannot in a letter begin to tell you the great number of things I would like to tell. There is too much and it is too complicated. I am pinning hope therefore that you may both come here to the east very soon. I have reasons.

I would greatly like to see you.
I may shortly have at my disposal a stately luxurious log house in the Ontario backwoods but not too far from focal points where I and wife would be delighted to have you both.
In the east there is much more possibility of turning a penny at something useful. There is quite a possibility that I could find some congenial work on films for either or both of you.

My plans are not yet quite complete but if they work out as I hope I will write again and ask very seriously for you to consider coming quickly. I will write in about two weeks and let you know how things stand. In the meantime I am conscious that you have asked many questions that I have not answered but bear with me a while and I will try to answer them I hope by word of mouth but if not by a more worthy letter than this. Treat this as a first slim installment, carrying to you both (commend me to Miss Bonner) my love,

Yours,
Gerald Noxon

3

Dollarton P. O.
Dollarton, B. C.
September 21, 1940

Dear Gerald:
Yours was most welcome and omnivorously read: many thanks. News here is as infrequent as on shipboard: when it does arrive one often feels his correspondent may be dead. Strange you should have been at Conrad's. All things return, the eternal return as Conrad, who writes nowadays with such gusto he must make many of the poets of our generation feel they have one foot in the grave, might say. It is refreshing to compare his later work with Eliot's later, the *Family Reunion,* etc., which is as necrophilic as ever. I believe that Conrad's early work sent one even further down the drain than Eliot's, if possible. The trouble even with Eliot's kind of drain is that it reeks of sanctity, whereas Conrad's honestly and majestically stank. I see no reason why one should not be lead down the drain: I believe it an important experience if the drain is fulsome enough. The long and short of it is: Conrad is a poet, in the sense that Shakespeare and Keats were poets. There is the same love of good and evil, that fierce glare which sent Eliot on all fours away from it into the church to keep his inhibitions warm, and Tolstoy gibbering into a station waiting room at three o'clock in the morning at the age of eighty or thereabouts, howling and spewing, and still certain, though it can have been but cold comfort to him, that *Uncle Tom's Cabin* (he was perhaps more unconsciously influenced by Eliza's escape over the ice cakes than by Lear's biding the pelting of the pitiless storm) was greater than *King Lear.* It must be admitted that Conrad doesn't give much of a damn about certain things. For my part (to oversimplify) I find him, as a poet, a more and better influence than he was to me at twenty. Much of his work has been heretofore shockingly underrated or fallen upon by pimps and rogues. This is very unfair, but all this will change. I think he has made a very fine marriage. I much admire both Mary and her work: that I should have, even in a very small degree, have assisted at this gives me much pleasure.
    Now, about going east. This is precisely what we strove to be able to do for many months. We found ourselves in a hateful position here, I won't go into details now, but later, if I see you, I perhaps will, for much, though it seemed tragic then seems amusing enough now: suffice it that, had not the possibility of going Conradwards burned like a beacon before our eyes, there would have been plenty in our lot difficult to bear.

While passing over many of these things that would have been difficult to bear I might mention this apprehension as the most personal & because it still exists: that one should proceed headlong into this war without first at least having taken one's bearings with one's friends. Since one is not in the first line of defense one ought to try to create the opportunity, and among British Israelites and Oxford Groupers here—I do not speak of those of course who have already gone, only of those who remain—this is difficult. Is it possible to be a pacifist and at the same time fundamentally bloodthirsty and hypocritical? That is how certain people here strike me. Rather more important than this is the fear that were I called up at present no provision would be made for Margerie, whom by this time you are aware of: not only no provision, but she would have no status. We cannot marry until October 15: even then there is no guarantee that, should I leave, she would be provided for. Every day I see in the paper some complaint from a woman whose husband is in the army: he has left her an allotment, but she has not received any money yet, even though he joined up on May 15th. It is true that Margie could get a job: but is it true? Margie would then be the wife of an Englishman, hence English and American, and an Englishman, that is a visitor, (or American) has no status, at least so far as a job is concerned. For instance I have not been allowed to register. When I applied to join up, no one even bothered to take my name. That is, as a soldier. Actually, my application to the Navy came to the same thing.

At the moment our situation is such. We have, not counting potentialities, about two hundred dollars. That sounds little: on the contrary, it is a fortune. Our rent costs us practically nothing: we hew our logs, draw our water: oil lamps and candles; and so forth. We cook, on a wood stove, such meals as remind us of Dijon. We have a boat, and so travel by water. Last Sunday I rowed fifty miles: why, I don't know, we have not looked at the boat for a week after that. Anyhow, there it is. With this money in hand, we were therefore able even to ask you down, without this being in the least a Mexican invitation. For it is possible to live as well as a king on next to nothing, a great deal better, in fact, than many kings I could think of. In addition to this there is a hope based upon a solid foundation that soon advances, or at least an advance, will be forthcoming on books. But my permission to remain in Canada expires October 31: Margie's on November 15, these permits having in the past already been renewed. Probably all that is needed to renew them is, as it was before, an appearance of opulence which can be simulated for ten minutes or so. Were I in Toronto it might be easier it is true. For my presence in Toronto at all would indicate that I had had at least enough money to get there from Vancouver and hence probably enough to remain. The question also arises: where, if I do not remain in Canada, should I go? Certainly not to the States. I do not expect there will be any difficulty, however, about remaining. Although I have been toiling with the prospect in view of existing quite apart from any funds I might get from England (for it looks as though these must be written off entirely in the future) when I read your suggestion that there was a possibility of work in Toronto, and at that upon films, and at that, possibly, with yourself, I rubbed my eyes. It is, of course, probably some kind of joke—too good to be true. However, in case it is not a joke it has occurred to me that I might really be able to lend some useful assistance. I can only guess at the kind of work you have chosen or which has chosen you and I am assuming that, if that work is upon documentary films, that you have to struggle against the form but at the same time accept it much as a poet no fool for iambic pentametres but committed to them has to struggle with them and against them: I have seen a great film about a duck, about an African lung fish, about Latter Day Saints in Utah. As for propaganda, good propaganda, I take it, is good art. (e.g. *The River*.) I have not seen the Hemingway film about Spain, but I did see one in Mexico called *España in Llames,* which made me go straight out and land in gaol. That similar results were expected from such films as *Storm over Asia*—I will never forget how you made the gramophone play, in the silver fox scene, Joe Venuti's bamboozling the bassoon—is presumably why they were not more widely distributed. Knowing nothing even though I had been a fireman at sea and through a Chinese Revolution at the time I first saw *The End of St. Petersburg,* I did not recognize it as propaganda at all. I merely thought, responding to it emotionally, that it was marvellous, the best I had ever seen (etc.) up to that point: the opening sequence of windmills on the steppes made me weep, as it were, "from the sheer beauty of it." In the same way, I was moved—or misled—by Alexander Room's *The Ghost That Never Returns,* of which I can, though I saw it only once and that eleven years ago, remember every detail. Anyhow, good propaganda, for whatever cause, is good art. *The Lion has Wings* would have done, I should have thought, damage to any cause, however noble. How many times and in how many English films do I have to see that bloody toy Spanish Armada, shot in a bathtub? There are a thousand things on this subject I would like to discuss with you: Paul Strand's *Redes,* Dovjenkho's *Frontier.* I will keep them for another letter or occasion. What I am trying to say is such great films have stormed in me day and night! One day I would like to assist you make one. Meantime, if you are not pulling my leg, may I suggest to you that even if there is some possibility of helping in some such meek capacity as writing the least important part of the dialogue for a film about icebreakers, that I feel you would not regret providing that opportunity. As for films about regiments, the best one I ever did see was a French one about the Foreign Legion—not by Renoir, Duvivier, or Feyder, the director had some triple-barrelled name which I have forgotten. The music was by Eisler, and it was called simply, in Mexican, *Una Aventura en Moroc. An Adventure in Morocco.* Have you ever seen such a film, and if so, who made it?

Our problem in any case would be to get to Toronto. Assuming the worst from our books, what money we have is nothing when one takes such things as fares into account, though a lot otherwise as I have tried to show. Perhaps you have some advice. *Our* invitation is still open, you know, but that sounds imposs. We might hitchhike.

At all events, it is not all impossible, if we ever get there, that you might find, in me, a Pudovkin in the Outhouse. Here's a health to your Thunder over Canada, whatever form it may take, then: Margie joins me in sending our love to you and Mrs. Noxon—

Que viva—life!
Malcolm Lowry

4

Dollarton P. O.
Dollarton, B. C.
Canada
November 2, 1940

Dear Gerald:

I was very glad to hear from you—and very much hope you do come here rather than go to British Guiana. Dollarton is fine, the Rockies are very fine, Vancouver itself is a lousy place that stinks to high heaven with hypocrisy; as does much of everything and everyone else. Our case is now somewhat "improved" in that, for some obscure reason, money has started to come from England: whether it hails from a forgiving old man, an elder brother suddenly heir to a forgotten investment of mine that thawed when no one was looking, or merely from some amiable eccentric, we have no way of knowing: it hails, however, from the Westminster Bank of Liverpool, which one had thought bombed out of existence long since, and is in the shape of 25 English pounds or $110 a month, to be continued until further notice. This now puts us in the position of being able to arrive in Toronto without feeling that we were imposing some kind of moral blackmail upon you by informing you we were there, and conversely, puts you in the position, should you arrive

here, of being able to visit the Cabinet of Dr. Caliglowry without any un-
pleasant sense of grinding the face of the poor.

Thanks for mentioning me to Grierson. It seems a long time since I
saw *Drifters* . . .

Is Len Lye over on this side, by the way?

Did you ever hear tell of one Karl Grune—a German Jew who years
and years ago in Germany made *The Street,* and a few years back made
Abdul the Damned in England, with Nils Asther? Neither of those films
are good looked at as a whole: both had genius, I thought.

Well: let us know what you are doing—here, as elsewhere, our morale
is "indescribable"—authoritative sources state,—nowhere do you find
people more keenly aware of the war than in Vancouver—two million
bayonets stand between us and the last quarter of an hour, and even the
lamp-posts stand ready to protect their "honor." We are very sincerely
hoping to see you soon, whether we come east or you come west. Love
to you and your wife,

Malcolm

5

Greenhill
Falls Church
Virginia, U. S. A.
[December 1940 or January 1941]

Dear Malcolm,

Have sent off your passport application to the mean sounding Jeacle.
God knows whether I will do as voucher as I have none of the official
qualifications. But I wrote a note saying that I had been at Cambridge
with you etc. I hope it works. If not we must try other means. My plans
have all gone phooey. Grierson has resigned as Canadian film commissioner and all my prospective jobs have evaporated for the time being
so I am working away trying to finish a novel in which I hope to interest
some New York publisher. This address is my wife's home where I am at
present sponge. It is very pleasant. I plan to be in New York towards the
end of this month to hawk my wares so let me know what your movements are going to be. I am in with permission to stay 6 weeks but if I get
some money from a publisher I will try and extend my visit for a while.
By the way as you are contemplating travel don't forget the possibility of

travelling by bus, it's incredibly cheap and also amusing. Hope we shall
see you,

Yours,
Gerald Noxon

6

Dollarton P. O.
Dollarton, B.C.
January 15, 1941

Dear Gerald:

Very many thanks indeed for so promptly getting me out of the Jeacle.
And your aid was entirely effective for I have just received my passport
all O. K. and countersigned by his henchman at Ottawa, one Mr.
Skelton. Sir Sparrowe has drawn a timid line through the Union of
Socialist Republics of Soviet Russia, otherwise it still seems valid everywhere from Penguin Island to baboon-occupied Dahomey. Thanks a million! All luck with the novel: I note what you said about bus traveling
and agree it is good fun, though my last experience was gruesome.
Though armed with a perfectly good visa and the right papers and all
when I set off in September 1939 to see Margie in the U. S. — to say, as I
thought, good-bye before going to England — I was turned back at the
American border as without proof that I would not be a public charge.
The law had changed between the time I got the visa and the time I set
forth. That happened to lots of people, including Canadians at that place.
They pick upon bus travelers particularly because they assume they
ought to be able to afford to travel by train if they can go to the U. S.
A hell of a note. And if you don't appeal within 48 hours you can't go in
for a year. Of course this was at the weekend, and with my G. H. Q. in
the States, I couldn't get the necessary dope in time. It was hellish. Do
you remember Alexander Room's *Ghost That Never Returns*? It was like
that only different and worse. It probably saved my life as a matter of fact
because I'd been fixing to go to England: but I didn't think of that at the
time. So Margie came up here: and here we've stayed so far. I am thinking of a poem at the moment, called The Englishman Turned Back at the
Border, beginning:

A singing smell of tar, of the highway,
Fills the grey Vancouver Bus Terminal,

Crowned by dreaming names, New Orleans,
Spokane, Chicago—and Los Angeles!
City of the Angels and my luck,
Where artists labor to insult mankind
With genius coeval to the age,
And city of my love come next Sunday.
Out of a flat-hung shop a sleeked puppet
Hands me my ticket and my destiny.

The blue exhaust speeds parting's litany.
Then, with pneumatic bounds, we herd the street.
The lights, symbolic, nictitate in day.
Cautious, but with mechanic persiflage
—Rolando's horn could no more strangely wind—
Past Chinatown and names like Kwong Lee Duck,
Our bus treads asphalt with the noise of bees,
By taverns mumbling of skidroad scenes,
Then double declutched my heart through neutral
And sang it into high for U. S. A.

It goes on, of course: or rather, comes back . . . It struck me as a bit of a brainwave to put the rhymes or assonances in reverse so that you got the effect of the streets and the past slipping away from you but at the same time being intermeshed and interwoven with the present. When the bus comes back the rhymes are the other way around . . . The bus that brought me back was full of cheer, and I, most unrelievedly, of beer . . . So much for buses. My God, what brackish bilge is this. Thought it might make a good Venuti tune, Esquirish, however.

Our plans are vague but for the present we are staying here. We still hope to see you and Conrad sometime soon though don't know how it can be managed. Do let me know where you are. If you are in New York and have time why not look up my old pal Jimmy (*Best Short Stories* 32, 33, 34, 35, ad lib) Stern, whose address is 20 E. 68th St., New York City, who is a hell of a fine guy and who I know would enjoy meeting you.

Well, thank you again Gerald, the best of luck with the book again, too, and all the best to Mrs. Noxon.

Malcolm

P. S. Sorry your film job's folded, & Grierson resigned as Film Commissioner. I heard him and Morley Callaghan speak the other day. I thought they were good! But it gave me a glimpse too of the kind of goings on you probably had to wrestle with . . .

LETTERS 7-28

Summer 1941 to May 1944

Noxon travelled several times across Canada in the period 1941-43; he was gathering script material for his two CBC drama series, *They Fly for Freedom* (30-minute docudramas based on the story of the Commonwealth Air Training Plan and broadcast weekly from August to November of 1941) and *Our Canada* (45-minute skits, broadcast weekly from November 1942 to January 1943; usually based on the experiences of Joe, a teen-aged boy learning about the impact of religion, government, finance, agriculture, industry, the arts, and other forces on Canada's development). It was during his research stints in the west that he was able to visit Lowry in Dollarton, seemingly about once a year in 1941, 1942, and 1943.

In 1961, in the lengthy tape-recording which he prepared for radio broadcast in Boston, Noxon recalled his first such visit two decades earlier:

> He was not an easy man to find there. I knew that he lived in a little shack on the shores of Burrard Inlet, but I had to find out from asking locals where this could possibly be, and it was only after some difficulty that I learned that it must be at Dollarton that he was living. I had no idea what to expect of Dollarton: it was a name on the map and that was about all, and it was very hard to get there. I believe it was by bus that I finally got to the store at Dollarton, which was, oh, perhaps a quarter or half a mile from the place where Malcolm lived. And I had to ask at the store, which was also the post office, and there, of course, Malcolm and his second wife, Margerie, were well known: they got all their supplies from the store and visited it almost every day. There was a path down through the forest—very large

trees and very wonderful forest growth—that led down to the shore from the little store; for the first time I really wondered whether I would find Malcolm Lowry at the end of this trip or not.

Finally, however, I did find him, living in a small shack built up on stilts at the front end, and sort of nestling into the steep bank of the forest at the back, a little two-room affair—at least one room and one very small appendage or second room in the back—no, it was to one side, as I recall; anyway, there were two rooms in the little cabin. There was a deck around one side of it, and then there was a dock, or rather a catwalk that Malcolm had constructed, built out over the rocks, so that a row-boat which he had could be kept out there free of the rocks at low tide and also where it was possible to swim from when the tide was up—the big tide, I remember on the occasion when I first visited with them—and I just wondered whether it would come up high enough to lift the whole thing, the whole place, bodily away and take it out into the inlet.

I had not intended to stay the night with them—I had no intention of doing so—but I became so fascinated with Malcolm's account of what he was doing, which was in effect writing *Under the Volcano,* that I stayed over, and we spent most of the night in discussing the book and its problems. He read me very large portions of it and was most anxious to know what I thought about it since he had been more or less out of touch with people who could sit and listen to him and in whose judgement he had a certain amount of faith. He had been working more or less in the dark.

Now at this time Malcolm's personal life seemed to have straightened out tremendously and he was working very hard on the book. I remember on the first occasion of the first visit he read me the very wonderful opening chapter of the book and asked me for criticisms about it and this was rather difficult for me to do because I had really no grasp of the work as a whole or of the extraordinarily significant part which this opening chapter was to have in the work as a whole.

However, we did discuss for many hours the very opening sentence of the book, and we re-wrote it together perhaps twenty times until it assumed the shape which it has in the novel today. The difficulty was—and this was the old difficulty as far as Malcolm was concerned—that he wanted a first sentence of such extraordinary and monumental nature, he wanted to include so much information, such a broad vista, such a broad picture, and all in one sentence, that I told him that this was simply unreadable the way he had put it down and —whereas it was quite clear to me and had been for many years that

Malcolm was never going to be a writer of simple, uncomplicated, sort of Hemingway-style writing—this was going a little bit too far. In effect, we broke down what he had originally written in one sentence into three, and we also, I think, clarified the purpose and intent of locating Quauhnahuac in relation to other parts of the world and so forth—giving it a geographic location which was not so hopelessly involved as it had been initially.

Well, in the same kind of way and during that visit we went over many other parts of the book which had, even at that time—and this would be, let me see, this would be . . . in 1941, the summer of '41, I guess—the book had achieved almost the shape in which it was finally published, or it had achieved the main features which it later was to show, although a tremendous amount of rewriting had still to be done.

Much of this was, in my opinion, not absolutely necessary, and I think one has to realize that while there was an admirable side to Malcolm's perfectionism about what he was writing, that sometimes he re-worked material to a point where it began to lose its vitality. This wasn't by any means always the case. I have known him to improve things immensely long after I had considered them to have been sufficiently worked over. There was no telling as to what the result would be: sometimes it was good and sometimes it wasn't.

Well, after that initial visit to Dollarton I kept in fairly frequent touch by letter with Malcolm, I kept in touch with the progress of the book, I returned to Dollarton on two other occasions and stayed there—once for two or three days as I recall—during which time we were taken up not only with the *Volcano* but also with other stories and projects which Malcolm had in hand, including a book the manuscript of which was eventually destroyed in a fire—"In Ballast to the White Sea"—which he read to me as far as he had done it, and another short story about experiences in Bellevue Hospital in New York called *Lunar Caustic,* which has, I think, survived, and, as I understand it, is to be published.

I felt very strongly, and I tried to press this viewpoint with Malcolm at all times, that he shouldn't get involved in quite so many things at the same time and that the thing to do was to finish the *Volcano,* which was already beginning to shape up as a novel of quite extraordinary quality. I was so afraid that he might not ever get to the point of finishing it that I put whatever influence I could to bear on his completing the book. (Noxon, 1961)

7

Dollarton P. O.
Dollarton, B.C.
Tuesday [Summer 1941]

Dear Gerald:

Please don't forget and Margie emphasises it to come to see us if you can when you return from good old surrealist Victoria—make sure you see the delirious rosebushes, the angry totems, and Aristotle peeling among the lobelias, not to say the gangrened statue of the Queen herself, looking rather constipated and decidedly bed-raggled—when we were there we stayed at the Hotel Windermere and sang, nobody had ever sung in the Hotel Windermere before, it was almost a calamity: it was very fine to see you, and if we can put on some sun, that would be good, one feels, as would a picnic on some such fine island as say, Jug or Dog or Pug or even Scug Island. I could see you were tired, (though in splendid form) and I am afraid I did not make you any the less so by reading vastly from my book, but I may be forgiven, I hope, when I remind you again you were my first editor and hence I look to you very earnestly for criticism, which was given and has already been most useful. I would not have troubled you had I not felt there was something very strange there, if slightly monstrous, and, if I may say so, though it didn't look like it at first, finally perhaps even your cup of tea. For the thing was partly conceived as a sort of preposterous five dimensional movie, a sort of Noxon Nightmare—believe it or not . . . But it is not to read you my bloody book of course, I, we, ask you to come, though I may trouble you in this regard sometime for the same honest reason, but because it is a pleasure to see you and because after making recordings you will find I hope some pleasure in inviting the soul here. So come any time you like and stay as long as you like, come unannounced, drunk, sober, or even leading a giraffe. Or even "the little fellow behind you." Who was he, by the bye? The man couldn't have meant you, who must be about six feet and so two or three inches taller than I, and he couldn't have meant me, who am not exactly little either, for it was me whom he addressed—and I know the fellow quite well because I'm always chasing would-be thieves off his balcony. "They're waiting," he said, "up there. Not for you, but for the little fellow behind you." What if he saw someone else, affable I am sure, but invisible, and for whom perhaps something else was waiting, up there? Or perhaps he has gigantism . . .

Margie sends love,
Malcolm

8

Trail, B.C.
July 19 [1942]

Dear Friends,

To begin so, sounds kind of corny but it's what I mean so let it stand. This is no "thank you" and yet it is. What I mean is that I want to thank you but at the same time I just want to write you a letter. I am a poor writer of letters, in fact in that capacity I stink to high heaven of incompetence. The result is that I write few and so the vicious spiral descends, each ghostly coil confirming my long standing lack of ability in this connection.

It has been an interesting drive to this place which, God knows why, reminds me of Sheffield. I was sorry to leave Vancouver and you and I would gladly again walk through those green serpentinous woods to your door making sure to step over the big log that lies across the path. I think, I don't know why, that I shall see you again before very long. It is more a feeling of "I must" than "I shall." I will remember the uneasy ascent of Friendly Island haunted by your previous and different visits. "It never looks the same again" but don't worry I was with you before when the fresh strewn grasses marked a grave and the tree stump was a totem. I was with you too when you looked through a narrow place into another world. I followed you too, through the maze of Vancouver streets to the Castle, through the periods of probation, conditional freedoms and concealments, through Oxford and Israel, to the shores of the Inlet. I have walked through the forest to your door and somehow that forest is a part of life that I would not willingly lose.

Of course, Malcolm I have known all along that you have what it takes but how could I have known that you would be so lucky and by luck I mean you, Margie, or no, it is certainly more than luck. Luck is a poor misdirected kind of thing and in both of you I feel no misdirection only the feeling of rightness and inevitability. I send you my love and when the tide comes in and brings you some offering try to pretend it comes from me.

Yours,
Gerald

9

Dollarton P. O.
Dollarton, B.C.
July 28, 1942

Dear Brother:

Thou leavest a gap in the woods, in the sea, at bus time and in our hearts. Thank you for your very fine letter—the dahlias came out when we read it. This being more of a dispatch to remind how delighted we would be if you get an opportunity to come hither again soon.

We have planted more dahlias over a bad patch, our boat has a new fine anchor—an axe—and a new rope and now dances at its moorings clear of munching barnacles.

We have made one of our rare trips to town, this time to see Eisenstein's *Alexander (Prospect) Nevsky*—miles and miles and miles away I persuaded Margie to go to the Pug Island Palindrome or somewhere which wasn't improved by a small boy with St. Vitus Dance in the next seat, about the only other member of the audience, and the fact that *Private Snuffy Smith* on the same program got somehow transposed into the middle of it and we couldn't tell the difference for a time. Orangeman—as that organ of male prostitution in journalism *Time* would say—Prokofieff made a very fine din and bell noises and there was twenty-five minutes of the most thrilling movie we ever saw but even making allowances for it being cut to hell it was a bit of a disappointment. Even taking dialectics and a new synthesis of contradictions and the fact that he always admired D.W. Griffith (us too) into account it was pretty sad. We simply couldn't get the intention, or if we did, the yards and reels of Laurel and Hardy, Marie Dressler and even Captain Flagg and Sergeant Squirt seemed to belie it, and it seemed mostly like a horrible regression, and we would be glad of your opinion. It took us twelve chocolate sodas, a carrot juice and the subsequent appalling hangover to drown ours.

Have been working very hard—both of us—since you left, and have wrought 100% improvements thanks to you, in the early pachydermatous prose of the *Volcano*. If ever you are in need of any of our ars est celowry artem it is of course proudly at your disposal from this end if any use.

I am sawing the succubus on the shore, but... Nature is the most beautiful thing I ever saw in my life. Our best loves to you and Betty,

Malcolm and Margie

10

[Dollarton, B.C.]
Tuesday, August 11 [1942]

Dear Gerald—
I'm not so good at letters either, but I just wanted to tell you how happy
your letter made us. It's astonishing what a big hole you left here after
such a short visit. There is no more news from us—we continue to work
hard, Friendly Island is still there, the tide still comes in every day, the
fallen logs still lie across the path through the forest. And here are the
snapshots we promised you. They were all taken last summer and the
house doesn't look its very best because the pier wasn't finished and the
verandah boxes weren't there yet, but the sea was, and so was the forest.
Do come and see us again, soon! And bring Betty with you next time.
                                        Much love from both—
                                        Margie

11

Dollarton P. O.
Dollarton, B.C.
September 15, 1942

Dear Gerald:
    Just a note to say you leave a gap. Forest, boats, islands etc.—even
cats—miss you. We look out for your radio program, what time the bat-
tery fades. Meantime work progresses apace; Margie's proofs should be
here any moment; you must come here sometime in September, not a
soul, the tide is always in, and there seem to be three full moons—All the
best to you & Betty.
                                        from Malcolm and Margerie

12

Dollarton P. O.
Dollarton, B.C.
October 29, 1942

Dear Gerald—
    I—we—thank you very much for sending the poems ["Branches of
the Night"] which are very powerful, original and dramatic and should,

if they are a touchstone of the whole, make an excellent book. In fact better than I have said. Above all, it is refreshing to listen to a poet who speaks in his own voice and not through a dictograph borrowed from Hopkins-Spender-Auden et al and who does not find it necessary to write in braille. (I may say in passing that I am not one of those who have objections to "obscurity" etc. in case my praise should seem to have a curse in it. But a semanticist within me is more comfortable if I can feel in the same room with the writer, or, if he happens to be Rimbaud, at least lying on the same pavement. In this case the reader does feel himself on the same blasted heath, in the same ruin.) We spent some exciting evenings reading and discussing them and I am sending you what emerges therefrom that might be useful, or constructive. Our opinions differed occasionally as to intention and meaning, but in the main we agreed, though I may start a few hobby horses of my own rocking a little later. First, though, I take it one is right in assuming that the "one day in the middle of my life" of the opening strikes the Dantesque note for a kind of Inferno. I think it is a very effective and deceptively simple opening. I think perhaps one would get along better if I took them separately, thus:

I. One's feeling was that the writer was going to play Virgil to the reader's Dante, and that there were not going to be any leopards, but right away a sun of some import setting. Since the sun never sets in the advertisement in the London magazine programs on the domain in question one has the sun placed and I take it that the poem is a sort of prelude and statement of the whole. The sense of helplessness in that case is as well conveyed as is that in the Prufrock poem by the etherized patient. I like the imagery, which again is deceptively simple: that the apparent fire caused by the sunset is analogous to the actual fire seems an obvious enough thought at first but the more you think about it in this context the less obvious it becomes. (One does not miss either that since the fire is cupped in the people's hand that the fire is something more and also something more than mere firebombs.) Again: "I heard the sight of heavy things / Falling in the night" seems at first merely an adroit way of conveying precisely that, but the more you think about it the more sinister it sounds. Actually the lines carry with them a sorrowful and dreadful weight, which explodes at just the right point in the reader's mind. I do not know either how you manage to make what is virtually an onomatopeia visual, but that is the effect. In short: this opening is a good deal more than merely "right."

IV. Some of the sidestreets can probably be counted on not to be sure of this poem at first, which is the way I like to feel. I do not like the delayed action bomb of the meaning to delay too long however, any more than I like to be blown to smithereens immediately. First of all I couldn't see any nexus between the opening lines and the rest of it but meantime there was a certain irony and bitter satire glancing off one and ricochetting here and there. Then we saw the dead man a'glowerin' at us and began to read it in different ways, each as good as the other; and each possibly wrong (or both possibly right) though I was very satisfied with my version. The poet asks the dead man wryly and bitterly and humorously the questions of lines 3, 4 and 5. And the dead man, in sepulchral monotone (as it were) gives his reply in the rest. Both questions and answers are dramatically pregnant with associations (cf. significance of fires with the fires in I). Margie had the poet as it were straightening up, after "any old bones" and declaiming the rest himself. At this point one only didn't feel stupid for not seeing the whole thing immediately because of the suspicion that one was supposed to see three whole things simultaneously. Anyhow, it has a very sinister, almost Chinese effect and it was not lost upon us that the "sidestreets" meant both more and less than sidestreets, and both less and more than "people." You felt that there were chords here that would be resolved later and one was certainly not disappointed in the scope of your selection. One felt too a curious satisfaction too in the poem as a separate entity, though I had pleasurable difficulty with the word "spent," which insists rebelliously on being attached to fires and in making an oblique and profound meaning—out of the attachment too of a contrary nature, even when it more obviously applies to "pots" etc.

V. The double exposure here too may leave some of your sidestreets cold but for our part this is a beautiful poem that makes a fine and mournful music. Neither the significance of the man with the band of gold nor what the dope-fed streets were, nor the peoples' face was, nor that the woods again were more than woods (possibly even the jungle) were lost on us. I think the chiasmas—is it chiasmas?—at the end is especially effective, and though I am at a loss for terminology just at the moment to approve your method, it seems again, more than merely "right." Somehow you make it possible for the reader to hold beautifully in his hand at the same time both the real city and the city in the pool . . .

VI. Here again was a deceptive simplicity. The things that are left after the bombardment, in the rooms exposed in the torn buildings, a bed, a stove, etc., have become as it were altars that mark where the people were sacrificed. Lares and penates. This makes "essential miracles" the more meaningful. (For another thing, in wartime "miracles" are essential in other respects too, both homely miracles of freak bombardments for the papers and other kinds.) The five and ten is Woolworths in England and since the woman hadn't a flag to hide her thighs, the scene of the looting might be taken to be an international one. Enter the sanctifying pimp—who might be taken as any governmental caucus of cranks and cravens—with his exploitation of the feverishness and thieving. The "woods" seem to link poem 5 to 6 here (jungle?). There is a suggestion of a new government in "proper respectable house," but since the hot winds are blowing in the oldest grange it is obvious the war is still on. If your intention was not merely to tell a simple story, it still makes a powerful and gruesome cartoon. But clearly its full meaning will only appear in relation to the other poems.

XIX. It is pleasant to see you really keelhauling a fat hypocrisy alongside your poetic vessel, and I hope you send some more overside. I feel that an objection might be raised to your use of the word aseptic, which does not—doubtless on purpose, and it achieves the right evocations—precisely mean sterile, but I don't see any way round it. Margie liked the honest anger in this one, and so did I, though it is about the only place where I seem to hear a voice not quite your own, the other voice doesn't come through clearly, but you do half sense a little Daylewis Auden poltergeist spendering around somewhere in the isherwoods, though perhaps this is only an illusion. I like its directness and intensity: though I was at first upset by the aldermen even being able to find the rubble of their lives in my conception of your woods.

XXX. We've read this so many times now it's become quite an old friend and we admired this poem of the falling plane very much indeed. "Bound to the crushing spiral / of the sky's intent" are terrific lines as are the ones preceding—"And then I saw an unremembered star / Falling to the wolves of centuries old / White to the black panes / of widowed night / a cross came Falling." The form substance rhythm imagery are all finely spun together. The only criticism is one of ourselves. Though its meaning sinuated and unfolded simply and beautifully as a stalk with an opening flower on the end of it, we were so on the lookout for possible gliding mysterious paratropes and floating parambiguities by this time that all of a sudden we became possessed of the notion that he hadn't, after all, landed safely (and all that that implied) and that the plane's supremity in the tangled aftermath suggested the supremity of death and rest for the pilot, and a crash instead of his plausibly having pulled out of the spin or at least pancaked magnificently or made a successful crash landing. (I hear groans from the stage at this point of Go out.) Of course what actually happened to the pilot is beside the poetical point, but what certainly led us off the track was our ignorance. How could he pull out of a spin with his ignition gone? we asked. Perhaps he could. But if not, you would know about it—so in that case perhaps the man bailed out, but no, that couldn't be, and so on, half the night we argued irrelevantly, until we came back to the original meaning again and did a two point landing into bed ourselves.

XXXIV. Noxon in Wordsworth (1805) mood—This hit, as the saying is, with a terrific impact. "Titanic cannot tell how deep / The chasms and the caves of night," has the same sombre reverberating [spondees] as some of the other lines I have mentioned (though there will always be some fool who thinks that Titanic is some sort of god or an image of a doomed ship thinking about an iceberg). Margie was carried away and had no difficulty it seems, but I had some about the "consummate masters of the briefest sea," since your use of "waves" and "wind" was so suggestive: for instance I couldn't be satisfied that the masters were the wind and sea only, for their personification is strangely carried out, and for "waves" and "wind" I had already substituted—detachably and interchangeably—in my mind, sea-forces, air-forces, so that what I saw holding past proud heads in shame were the men themselves, possibly on both sides, and possibly you intend that some such inchoate emotions should blow up from your theme to your reader standing on his cliff like spray from thundering surf below and then occasionally that he would be blinded as with salt. "On insurrection shore no new thing grows" bothered me for analogous reasons, since insurrection suggests an immediate rising up against civil or political authority so that I kept thinking still of waves, only this time differing somewhat emblematically, rising up against cliffs. I get your point, however; I feel, though, I could stand enlightening on some others. The incantatory remainder of Noxon's poem conveys with nervous power the sense of stunned gloom that (as the *Times Literary Supplement* might say)—The sarcastic ending is odd, and I guess, true, and probably right. Margie liked the first and last poems the best.

Generally speaking, though naturally I realise that difficulties one might have with the item may disappear with the mass and everything is qualified by this, I feel, if I may say so, that in a few cases the ambiguities seem to spring less from the necessity to express several layers of meaning (though there is this too, of course, sine qua non) than from some infectious necessity caught from the contemporary climate merely to be "ambiguous." It is true it wouldn't need to be contemporary, one might have caught it from Rimbaud or Hardy or the Holy Bible, but the point is the bug I am thinking of is more a critical bug than a poetical one. A poet like Herrick, let us say, achieves certain unconscious ambiguities here and there and say, Richard's [Richards'] Bill points them out. It isn't that Richards [sic] Bill isn't a poet too in his way so much as that the person who passes the bug on has caught it from R.B.'s criticism and not from Herrick and that the bug thereupon nips you in the critical apparatus when you come to write your poem with the result that sometimes you find yourself writing the poem less for the poet-critic in yourself than to satisfy some kind of (at the moment) ideal critic outside. I went on at length about this, dragging in everyone from Stefan Georg to Jesus Christ, and came back to the subject. I feel that when you personally are most "apparently" simple you are most effective, and also there is more "thickness" of meaning, "ambiguity," if you like, in the best sense of that exhausted word, that is what you say seems *truer* on more levels. When you are being more overtly and consciously ambiguous, on the other hand, the conflicting meanings some times produce a kind of "dislocation of affects" that weakens the poem. It is as though you had deliberately plunged a perfectly good line at heart in alizarin—or is it anthraquinone?—and dyed it a different hue. Having said this I can't immediately find a good example, but I am going to let the criticism stand, perhaps because it sounds good, or perhaps because I feel that though it may be invalid in the case of these poems there is here and there, a *threat* of your doing something of the kind. I don't say it mightn't sometimes be cunningly done, of course. Anyhow, I'm all in favour of one who gives up all attempts to hijack the sadistic but essentially pantywaisted zeitgeist and who leaves all the pansy boys (doubtless engaged now in some "poetry of clarification" though it's the same old absomphe, you may be sure) to their solidarity and—incunabula was coming into the next sentence, so I'll quit: but in short, starts something of his own. Which is, I believe, in the main very much what you are doing, from what you have sent us: so all power to your arm! If the idea hasn't occurred to you already, might I venture to suggest that you include in the "Branches" three or four perfectly strict (not that yours are not strict according to their own special strictness) formal poems, the old abbaabba, a sonnet or two, even trotting out the barrel organ, if necessary—I seriously think the contrast would be very effective and might serve to buckle tighter the surcingle wherewith you bind your theme. Even a sestina might be a brainwave—(I was thinking of Dante's in the *Vita Nuova*) a brainwave because so it seemed to me, you could then make magnificent play with 6 of your most important symbolic words—say: sun, fires, woods, streets, night, cliffs, since not rhyme but repetition of end words characterizes the form, the end words of the first line being repeated in an order which lets the last end word of each stanza be the first end word of the next, the sequence being 123456, 615243, 364125, 532614, 451362, 246531, there is a three line envoy which has three of the terminal words at the ends, the others earlier in the lines (just in case you haven't been slap through your thesis on the sestina very lately)—well, it was just a notion, perhaps not so silly as it sounds.

Thank you very much for the photos which were delightful with some entrancing pictures of Betty and Nick [Noxon's wife and son]... We look out for your program on the radio... Shall we send the poems back, or are they in the nature of a copy it might be insurance to let us keep, for the duration anyway apart from our liking to have them?... We had them all ready to send back, then decided to wait your word. We would also very much like to see some more.

The weather is radiant with mill wheel reflections of the sun on water turning and sliding down the house, in which Nunki, our cat, has lately seen a ghost. I'm pretty sure it was a ghost and it was sitting in your chair. We saw Nunki behaving oddly about the chair and we put her in it three times and each time it was as if she'd had an electric shock and she shot straight up about four feet into the air. We decided it was a good ghost that was helping but didn't like cats, and since its departure we've rather missed it.

It's too bad about Betty's citizenship, but I have a hunch that it will straighten itself out shortly all right. We sincerely hope so. There was a case here of an American who'd enlisted in the Canadian army and had been discharged as medically unfit and who not only lost his American citizenship but was unable to get back across the border; but I heard that had been straightened out.

We've been presented with a wreck: or rather it wasn't a wreck. We woke up one morning to find a boat full of water trying to moor itself to our pier—about a twenty footer, ironbound, absolutely covered with seaweed and polyps—and with only one small hole in it, it's impossible to find out the owner, and we're thinking of salvaging it, putting a motor and a sail in it and who knows—one far off day—sailing to the Happy Isles therein.

We had an airmail post-card—delightful medium!—from Conrad, who seems in good form but busy—and by the way, did you get our snapshots? There's no other news with us: we're both working hard, Margie has started a new novel and I'm finishing the *Volcano*. Do write when you have time—we look forward to your letters. Best of love to yourself and Betty and Nick.

Malcolm & Margie

13

Dollarton P. O.
Dollarton, B.C.
January 15, 1943

Dear Noxons:

My name is Inarticulacy:—

You should not have—but since you did—herewith an expression of inadequate gratitude, the fear that it could not but be inadequate being the cause of my, our, having delayed till now to make it.

The picture, Betty, is marvellous, and stormes in our room day and night, and we are very proud indeed to own it. One seems to see somehow in the driftwood a calamitous battle of marine monsters or of creation divided against itself. At the same time one seems to hear an inhuman cackling of scales and spines as of cactus in the plains of Yucatan. Since I understand that even so it is but a detail perhaps I may presume to judge, as from a synecdoche, the greatness of the whole. (Nor does the Melvillean whiteness of the frame escape one.) And the picture gets better, if possible, all the time as one lives with it.

I wish you could see, Gerald, how much the room is improved by its presence, but I won't go into that, since this must be short.

I wish you could both be here for we seem to see potential pictures for Betty everywhere and moreover we are putting on some magnificent freezing blue weather with the sun raining diamonds in Burrard Inlet and sea-gulls and the washing frozen on the line and a two hundred foot alder plunging above the house like the mast of a ship on a rough day in the Indian Ocean. Whenever we have a day of this kind we always say: "It's a pity Gerald couldn't be here to see this." If we have another kind of good day: "This is rather like that day Gerald was here," rather as if we were Indians and time were measured from the day the WHITE MAN came. "Now when the WHITE MAN was here um—"

I hope you didn't suffer much damage in the storm that hit your part of the world. One heard grisly reports of hens frozen in their tracks and lines down and power cut off and God knows what and one was alarmed lest you might be affected.

Please tell me whether or not to send your poems back. What was said of Betty's picture as to "storming in one" applies here likewise. On subsequent re-reading I felt some of my remarks were probably a little stupid. But they were meant to be constructive as to the work in progress. One certainly looks forward to an excellent book.

Our radio irreparably and disappointingly gave out on the fourth installment of *Joe* [*Our Canada*] so I have no very useful comments here since one cannot do justice and also since I have no touchstone to guide me in criticism in that line. What I heard often moved me but I am not quite sure if for the right reasons and am not sure either whether a certain personal loyalty doesn't interfere in this case with one's objectivity, the case not being primarily, so to speak, one of aesthetics. Perhaps the most useful thing I could say is that everyone I have spoken to about it seemed enthusiastic.

We work very hard here. No word from Conrad at all in months. Hope he's all right.

And here's to the next visit of the WHITE MAN—and may he upon that occasion, if possible, bring the WHITE WOMAN (to whom renewed thanks) too.

Love,
Malcolm & Margie

14

R. R. #1
Unionville, Ontario
March 14, 1943

Dear Lowrys:-

It's with shame as usual that I finally sit down to write a fearfully over-due sort of letter which I feel can never catch up with the intentions of the many carefully composed but never written down in the early sleepless hours in pullmans. The equipment of pullmans with dictographs would, I feel open up an entirely new era in expression but then . . .

Anyway, I'm glad you liked the picture. *The St. Louis Blues* to my eternal sorrow arrived in little bits—an awful shame—I hate to write it down as I feel that precludes the possibility of the record re-assembling itself à la reversed motion pictures, an event which I have attempted to induce by refusing to throw away the bits.

I have been on the move ever since *Joe* finally got finished. I've been in New York on two separate trips, Washington and CAPE COD. Betty and I spent the best part of a week with Conrad and Mary who are in great form and more prosperous than for many a day. We took a friend from England—Laurence Gilliam by name of the BBC who has been in New York with us and there were three other guests including a lady recently released from a loony bin. So it was a real Aiken party with rivers of gin and oysters, clams and movies. Very enjoyable except that I had to have a horrible attack of sinus trouble in the middle of it all which completely laid me out. Betty is at present in Washington with Nick in order to avoid the balance of this very severe winter. It has been no joke out here with snowbound roads and so on but it looks as if it may be over if the present thaw holds for a few more days. B [Betty] has a job in the book department of a big Washington store which keeps her in funds (I can't send her a nickel from here) but she will come back for the summer. In the meantime I am entirely on my own which is good for work but bad for fun. Not that it will last for long as I have a new series of programs for BBC and CBC combined which will force me to start travelling again very shortly. In fact it is just possible that the WHITE MAN will get as far west as the shores of Burrard Inlet in his search for buffalo. I hope so and I will know for sure within the next few days. If Vancouver is included in my itinerary I will probably fly there direct and arrive within a couple of weeks. You may be sure that I will keep you posted.

The release from a weekly radio show has been very welcome and I have been able to get on with other things to some extent in spite of my trips to the States. I'm at work finishing a short novel or rather long short story which I began in Rome some twelve years ago. It bears absolutely no relation to present day events, carries no message in particular and is therefore restful to work at but I haven't the least idea what to do with it when it's finished as it will fit no sort of publishable form—about 30,000 words and not very formal at that.

How goes the *Volcano*? I've been watching for signs of Margie's mystery but have seen nothing of it so far. Can I have missed it? I hope not.

About "Branches of the Night." I was more than grateful to have your very full and amazingly understanding letter of many months ago. On the whole you seem to have understood the poems to a degree which I had scarcely hoped for, in that the imagery and symbolism is not exactly of universal experience and in writing them I aimed to do no more than express myself to something beginning to approach my own satisfaction. In other words they are personal works and any degree of significance which they may have for others I regard as pretty fortuitous. I think there is very little in the poems I sent which you have not got hold of but of course you lacked connecting links as between I & IV for instance where the continuity is quite important. Still I was anxious to see how passages separated from the context would stand up on their own and I must say your remarks gave me a great deal of encouragement. Conrad's reaction was much as I had expected and thoroughly justified. He wanted more form and less loose ends. I am in theoretical agreement but that unfortunately does not seem to be the way my mind works, when it does work and I'm not prolific enough to be choosy.

I hope to be able to write in a few days saying that I'm coming your way.

all my love,
Gerald

15

[Birthday Card for Gerald Noxon]

[Dollarton, B.C.]
May 3, 1943

Trumpets sounding for you from the Wicket Gate—luck with *Teresina*—luck with "Branches" (let us see more)

May you have fair winds, strange and rich landfalls, and a good time. You will. All the best to Betty and Nick

—Bello, bello, il mare!

Arrivederci!

Malcolm and Margie

16

Snider Estate
R. R. #2
Oakville, Ontario
June 6, 1943

Dear Lowrys—

I'm afraid this doesn't stand much of a chance of developing into a full fledged letter as, although I am very much settled in here now, the CBC has flooded me with a mass of work on international programs which weighs heavily. In fact all seem to conspire to prevent my getting on with *Teresina Maria* which irks me exceedingly. However, some progress has been made and I intend to inflict some new chapters on you via air mail, alas, at no very distant date. In the meantime I enclose something which I found in Halifax which will give you some idea of the fantastic story of Sable Island. I found the little map in a ship-chandler's on Water Street and I think you will agree that it is something of a curiosity. In fact I know of no more amazingly suggestive document in connection with men and ships—suggestive and at the same time tantalizing. What, for instance happened to the *Ocean Traveller* left the Island Oct. 8th, 1870? What story is concealed by the cryptic "(lost)"? And what of the *Hard Times* that struck in 1811, the *Vampire, Bob Logic, Blonde, Pegasus, Boys,* and *Blooming Youth*? Someday I would like to try and find out.

Well, we have been hot and are cold again. I have been in Halifax, Montreal, Quebec City and so on and we are now very comfortably and satisfactorily settled in a large and rambling house on the lake. We are surrounded by woods full of trilliums and May Apples and by gardens of decrepit grandeur. Would that you could visit us. We have rooms and beds galore and 42 armchairs, mostly rockers. The place belonged to "Old Judge Snider" who died three years ago and bullied his extensive family unmercifully to the very day of his death. In order to prevent any rejoicing on the part of his family upon his demise he devised a will so full of trickery, double-entendus, that fierce inter family litigation still goes on with no prospect of settlement till all are dead themselves. In the meantime we are getting a lovely place upon which the judge squandered his misplaced affections. He was a dendrophilist and we benefit accordingly in the profusion of unlikely imported trees and shrubs all somewhat unkempt but none the less attractive for that.

I hope all goes well or even better and that your works proceed apace. Do let us hear when you can spare the time.

Yours,
Gerald

17

Dollarton P. O.
Dollarton, B.C.
June 15, 1943

Dear Gerald—

Many thanks for yours—did you get our birthday card by the way?—with the Sable Island thing. Blimey, what a romantic story. It's the most exciting thing I've heard of—I suppose Sable Island is *the* original Isle of Lost Ships of legend. We counted 83 ships piled up to port and 112 to starboard, 195 all told. Yes: *Bob Logic* and the *Hard Times* and *Blooming Youth* and the cryptically "lost" *Ocean Traveller* are about the most tantalizing, as you say: but what about *Reeves* (1876)? And *Inglewood* (1894) strikes near home. Then way up at the north end, on the left, you have the *Worchester* (1899); while far down on the left you have the *HATTIE C. Worchester* (1890). Then on the right *Echo* (1827) and on the left, as if responding to it nineteen years later the *LADY Echo* (1846). And what about the Rabelaisian brigantine, *Farto* (1875)?

> —Oh, we are the lads of the Farto
> And we just don't give a bloody farto
> So we never become disconsolato
> Oh, the Farto's lads are we!

One would like to live on Sable Island for a few months after the war and write a book containing 195 chapters, one for each ship.

We look forward exceedingly to seeing more of *Teresina Maria* and hope you will send some chapters soon. It is going to be a very grand book. But you must put in Musso's tennis game and a dark (or bright) transitional bit in mid-Atlantic. You are undoubtedly right, that it should end in tragedy, yet in that case don't you think Roberto should grapple a little more, kick against the pricks so to speak, toward the end. Granted that Teresina is your protagonist—all the same I feel Roberto has some nobility in him. I think you want to feel, when he comes to the U. S., that he has a choice, that he doesn't *have* to end in the gutter, and that he is aware of that too; on the other hand you know perfectly well all the while that he's going to. It isn't perhaps so much nobility as a sort of physical instinctive thing about him. But I believe you want to get a certain feeling of *waste* about his death, not just that Teresina's well rid of him, though of course I see her love for him is more the point. I think the contrast between Rome and Detroit or wherever will be terrific. But perhaps you'll be doing well if the chapters we see get as far as the picture or the seduction incident. What about "Branches"? May we see some more? I don't think you'll have the slightest difficulty in publishing them, when you want to. What about *New Directions*? But perhaps you don't relish being the Poet of the Month and that kind of thing? Perhaps the wisest course is to let them simmer till you've finished *Maria* and then get Schuster or whoever takes that to put them out next. Meantime you can add a few more to round it off. We suddenly got *Horse in the Sky* off in a great hurry and burst of glory—we're vastly pleased with it; took nearly all your suggestions and it seemed just right, so we got on the horse and bang. The *Volcano* smoulders to a finish in reverse, first chapter last, and will inflict it on you eventually with your permission. Am looking forward to getting down to the so-called Paradiso part—am full of ideas for it. Well, it's very beautiful here—a little more spring-like than when you were here last year, though we've never had a day as perfect as the one when we all walked to Deep Cove. You go to the store through a triumphal arch of salmonberries. While the other evening there was a grey ship with yellow riding lights lying at the oilwharf and behind it the grey smoke of a train and the grey-green hills and silver grey cylinders of the oil refinery and up above a moon in a blue sky with Venus alone burning hard in daylight, and then the smoke of the train going eastward to meet the smoke of the shingle mill, the grey smoke of the shingle mill hanging in the air mingled with the smoke of the train, and reflected, white, in the water; then afterwards the swift wash of another ship, like a great wheel, the vast spokes of the wheel whirling across the bay. And all these things with ourselves look forward to the next visit of the WHITE MAN.

I have a lot more to say, but Margie has gone to town for the day and there is major disorganization here: half a hard boiled egg in the sink, a shoe on the window sill, I have just dropped my cigarette case down the john, and I have been attacked by a pileated woodpecker—

With best love to Betty, whose picture we admire without end, Nick and yourself—from us both.

Malcolm

18

[Dollarton, B.C.]
September 7, 1943

Dear Gerald:

We've been meaning to write "The White Man" for a long time have in our heads many compendious letters—many thanks for yours of 25th July—but minor baffling harassments have put us off so far: no proofs of the *Shapes* [*The Shapes That Creep*], stupid reports on the *Horse* [*Horse in the Sky*]: we have made the acquaintance of a magician ("the only thing for which there seems no rational explanation is sprites")—we listen to your voice on the radio Mondays with enjoyment—it comes out from under the bed you slept on now: we don't use it, scarcely turn it on at all save for you & anyway it's broken—yes Mussolini being down the drain ought to help *Teresina* which haunts tremendously—we had been looking forward to some more MSS before writing?? Don't shrink the "Branches" too much—first thoughts often best. Am still ill apparently but getting better. We are going on a picnic to-day as it were with you.

Love to Betty & Nick
God Bless (Writing)
Malcolm & Margie

19

Dollarton, B.C.
September 28, 1943

Muy querido hombre blanco y noble:

Is your aunt in the garden with her strong stout stick? Escruch is an old man. He lives in England in a big house. Old (viejo). Big (grande). The house (casa)—I give up; but the Latins must go through it too . . . Many thanks for your letter from the Yukon and feel guilty at so scanty a correspondence from this end. You have not been far from our thoughts, however. After a foul summer, and with everyone gone home, we have had a sublime Indian summer, like spring, all of a sudden; endless days of sunlight. We re-visited the float where we ate lunch that day and like a signal the siren went off again, just as before. We have discovered other bays and crannies you must visit with us, notably a sunny cove on the dark side of the inlet. There are some queer isolated houses built on this side that get no sun in summer till five o'clock in the afternoon, and then only for an hour or so, though it is bright down by the water and we climbed up the cliff and found in the forest a tall lonely ruined house of four stories with a great wrecked fireplace and on the topmost floor, a square grand piano. You can imagine the strange chords that wind and rain must play there in the winter storms.

> Here [sic] him play
> That sinister melody
> That's what the people say
> When they hear those weird chords
> The mice run out of the worn out boards
> To hear him play
> That sinister melody . . .

Your Donneish poem is very amusing; but Donne's new pseudo popularity via Hemingway is as you say food for thought, suggesting some such as the following:

Donne he's regular

> Once more thou art the rage oh good John Donne
> Once more Oh Donne hast thou set sail for Spain
> Once more thy fame as at the Cheshire Cheese

But now a greater cheese has called thy praise
Ah little thought'st thou, among the Anabaptist Germans
That plump shadow boxers would quote thy sermons
Puffing down the Boulevard Saint Germain saying
                              "son of a bitch" . . .

We have had some other long picnics when we wished you were with
us, and on one we found a beautiful sunken blue canoe called *Inter-
mezzo*. Life has thus been very fine on the paradisal side—but a bit
daunting on the work side. Scribner's seems to have postponed Margie's
Shapes again and the first reactions on the *Horse* were superficially so
discouraging that I feel convinced that the book must be even better than
one had thought it. From the agent we have had no reaction at all but one
publisher thought it was "handled with facility but not significant
enough for present time," someone else thought it was not improved by
the "trick ending," (there is no "trick ending") but might have been a
better book if part of the second half was not so dull as the first, while
Margie's mother, which was the unkindest cut of all, apparently thought
that it was not only a bad book but was very nearly the worst book she
had ever read and went off into a nervous decline about it all summer and
(since she had felt she ought to be the heroine) refused finally to write
Margie at all and has only just come round to doing that again: no one, so
far, has judged it by its intention, or its form . . . As a consequence your
kind remarks, which I feel are true, were taken to our bosom. It will
make the grade in the end though, as you say; I am sure of that; but I am
filled with misgivings meantime that there is far less independence of
judgement on this side of the water than one would think; they have to
wait for some ratification or other to be imported by boat still.

There are queer and unique difficulties that ever beset the transplanted
too—which somewhat upsets this argument (and to get somewhat off the
subject and in a bracket)—why should not Conrad, for instance, have
made more of a mark in England? He had as much to say to us of value as
Eliot, I should have thought, if not more. Again why should Melville
have been always more or less popular in England and neglected in
America? On the subject of Melville: Margie gave me a collected
Romances and I read, for the first time, *Redburn*, the chronicle of Melville's first voyage on a ship called the *Highlander* that sailed from New
York to Liverpool. It is all about Liverpool in 1840 and there is one
obscure statue in an obscure square he noticed and chronicled (though in
1940 he suggests it will be no longer there) that was always a favorite
place of assignation near my father's office of my brother's and myself,
and I also described what it looked like in 1940 in "In Ballast" ["In Bal-

last to the White Sea"]. The actual ship that Melville sailed in *was* called the *Highlander* it is known and about this time you kindly sent me the graveyard of the Atlantic thing about Sable Island which I have been poring over with excitement ever since. Could it be—impossible!—but it was. Three quarters way up Sable Island on the right I found *Pegasus* (1830) *Crofton Hall* (1900) *Hope* (1828) *Highlander*! (1874). The *Highlander* was new when Melville sailed on her and his return voyage took him into those waters which she apparently plied fairly regularly: forty years is no great age for a sailing ship, so this might be a bit of a discovery. To continue in this Believe it or Not vein, somewhat prior to this Margie had asked me to produce some rather foolish sounding American town in Montana or wherever for the *Horse* and I was looking through the Atlas, always in hope of finding too, for reasons I shall explain, where Pope County was. The reason was this, that I had one New Year's day in Vancouver here been accosted by a drunken man who informed me: "I'm from the County of Pope. What do you think? Mozart was the man what writ the Bible. You're here to the *off*, down here. Man here, on the earth, shall be equal. And let there be tranquillity. Tranquillity means Peace. Peace, on earth, of all man—"

And so I wondered vaguely where Pope County was, for I had popped this man and his miraculous (at least to me) dialogue into the last chapter of the *Volcano*. But I had never found out where Pope County was. However this time looking through the atlas for Margie I turned to Minnesota. The first town that struck my eye was, in the County of Koochiching, a *town* named "Margie." Then my eye fell on another town, south of the Lake of the Woods but with no towns between it and "Margie," named "Malcolm." It was at this point I discovered also, far southwest, the County of Pope, and in it, two towns fairly contiguous, the one named "Starbuck," the other: "Lowry"! Starbuck is one of the chief characters in *Moby Dick*. Verily there are more things in heaven and earth, Horatio! But I think it is that there are intelligences in the void that sometimes like to amuse themselves at our expense, and feed our delusions of grandeur.

Which might bring me to our magician friend I told you about but perhaps I will tell you about him in our next. But meantime you might try your imagination on a conversation going on between Whitey and the magician (*not* a stage magician but a real one, right out of the 12th century, the greatest living cabalist, no less) in our shack, something on these lines:

—Aw it's a crummy set-up, it's the bloody set-up.

—and I said to this wizard friend of mine, oh of course he was strictly on the up and up, lived on the plane of Jupiter: I had invoked sulpher, you know, and banished earth—

—the bloody set-up, yis, that's it—

—on the plane of Mars, I think I was, by that time, let me see, and I said to this wizard, now about these elementals that have been bothering me lately—

I see, alas, that I shall have to catch the post. Let us see *T. M.* [*Teresina Maria*] when you have it. We're dying to see it. Sorry you're having trouble getting *T. M.* typed. Margie would have offered to do same for you save that it seemed impractical at this distance, but let us know if you get stuck and she'll rally round, she says to say, did before, but bafflements inhibited my writing.

How are the "Branches" coming? They should make a great mark, if you let them. If you find the prospect of sending them round too grim why do you not send them to us when you have them in shape, being careful to keep copies, etc., and let us bear the burden of the few inevitable stupidities on our souls. We would be glad to. Permanently to alleviate suffering, first dart a few added pangs! say I.

Well do try and come here—since you're so near and yet so far in Edmonton— is there a merry devil there?

We look forward to seeing you sometime again anyhow.

Best love to Betty and Nick.

God bless,
Malcolm & Margerie

P. S. I bought Nick a birthday card, as from Leo, but didn't send it because I got the idea then he might feel under some obligation burdensome to him to reply. Methinks I think too much.

M [Malcolm]

20

Dollarton, B.C.
November 14, 1943

Salutations to the White Man:

This is not in the general line (sic) [cf. Eisenstein's *The General Line*] of correspondence but is one pro Margie re *Horse In The Sky*, this long-suffering and admirable animal having now suffered more we feel undeserved punishment than the one in Raskolnikov's dream; she wondered if she might ship it to you in the form of a carbon with a view to your looking it over and seeing if its points appeared as sound to you as when we read and collaborated on it all together last spring and if anyhow you might have some advice on the subject. This we meant to do as soon as she had it completed but I had the bad idea it might win the Harper's Prize so it went off there and the carbon to Hollywood, the other fairly complete copy being already ripening for damnation in the hands of Margie's mother.

Since then the comments upon it have been of such a peculiarly blood-stained nature and Margie's relations with the publishing world suffered such Kafka-like permutations, that lesser victims might well have reached the end of their wit. Had Margie's agent not given up writing to her long ago in spite of impassioned appeals save vicariously in the form of moronic rejection slips I might be able to give you a more complete report. But what seems to have happened is that (1) Scribner's, after five promises that she was to have the proofs in a fortnight, seems to have postponed the publication of *The Shapes That Creep* indefinitely; (2) that Margie's other mystery *The Last Twist of the Knife* has not even been shown by her agent to Scribner's in spite of many appeals and has been making the rounds (several times) under the imprint of one mysterious Bonner Lowry, because her agent feels it would not be a good idea for two mysteries to come out in the same season, presumably 1967, under the same byline and for the same reason it has seemed better also to let it be known that this Bonner Lowry is a sort of man; (3) that *Horse in the Sky,* though not quite by this same Bonner Lowry, has been submitted, not to Scribner's whom one might have thought interested in the versatility and productiveness of Margerie Bonner, as the first novel of a kind of Englishwoman, a namesake and also thus coincidentally by name of Margerie Bonner, whose mysterious ambition it is to write short stories under the influence of Phil Stong about the Middle West.

Of course we have put our foot down, but then one might as well put it down in the middle of the Atlantic ocean at this distance; well, the mysteries will doubtless look after themselves in due course but the comments upon *Horse in the Sky,* which has so far been rejected by Harper's, Houghton Mifflin, Doubleday, Doran and William Morrow, have been of the following nature:

(A) It is written with facility but it is not significant enough for publication at the present time.

(B) The background is interesting but the story seems to us a little too melodramatic to be convincing.

(C) It would be a better book if the last half were as good as the first. She uses many adjectives.

(D) I think this book is sketched rather than written. I don't believe any revision could help but I wouldn't be surprised to see it emerge in another form in another book some day. The ending of Thurles and Dungarvon is really quite funny, when it is meant to be tragic. She is one Englishwoman who can write about America (I don't believe I would have known her to be English but "swine" at the fair stopped me.)

(E) The sales manager, myself, and the advertising manager, and the manager of one of the good Womrath bookstores all agreed it was unfinished and incomplete. Maybe it is an unfortunate sense of humor, but everyone here thinks the ending is funny, but not intentionally.

(F) The ending is magnificent, the descriptive passages are fine, but there are many gaps in the manuscript. We do not see our way to publishing it as it stands. However, we are very interested, and if she's ever around and hungry you tell her I'll take her to lunch with much pleasure.

(G) It has a trick ending—etc. etc.—

My own opinion, which I consider hard boiled and objective is that it is a kind of classic and would establish itself as such if published. Its façade is deceptively innocent and perhaps not enough precaution is taken against the wrong reaction of the reader but it succeeds in its intention and is a formally beautiful and complete work of art. I feel objectively I would say something like that if I were a publisher's reader and had never heard of its author from Adam's off ox. But if we send it along to you, could you read it some evening when you aren't too busy and let us have your final opinion of it as a finished product? And if you still think it is as good as you did last spring, perhaps you'd give us some advice on it???? And if you don't think so, will you please say so?

And now the mail is going so in haste—What about the poems and *Teresina?* Let us have *Teresina*. Do not forget my offer about poems. Your radio broadcasts are listened to with enthusiasm. Hope you got back safe from the Yukon and that you received our telegram and letter sent to you at the Edmonton address. We still remember that you *might* be out this way this winter and hope for news of that too.

Best love from us both to you and Betty and Nick—

Malcolm & Margie

21

R. R. #2
Oakville, Ontario
November 17, 1943

Dear Lowrys:-

Thanks, thanks for the letter. I should so much have written but I was hoping to get some favorable news from your end first. Anyway, please do send the *Horse in the Sky*. I'm particularly anxious for Betty to read it quite cold. She worked for a while in the book dept. of Woodward and Lothrop a big department store in Washington and has quite an idea of what sort of books people do actually buy. So her view may well be interesting. Not that I think there is an alteration to a book of that kind that could possibly be done. It is too right to be alterable and I think it must stand or fall as it is. However I shall be most interested to read it again after this interval. As for the readers' reports—it is only necessary to consider the publishing history of any good book. It invariably reads like a passage from *Alice in Wonderland*. I suppose at the moment publishers are even more than usually imbecilic in their comments as they are all trying to cash in on the war. A clever publisher at this moment would do well to publish no war books whatsoever and concentrate instead in building up a list of fiction that has some chance of becoming literature.

I have time for no more now as I have a broadcast crying out to be finished. Please send the book as soon as you can. All our love,

Gerald

22

R. R. #2
Oakville, Ontario
December 13, 1943

Dear Lowrys—

I've been trying to find time to write a proper letter ever since the *Horse* arrived but it has been a bit difficult as I have been doing two broadcasts a week for the last six weeks and I find that what with going into town twice a week I don't seem to have a minute to spare. I wish I could work in the evenings but I simply can't do anything except read and at that I'm half asleep by nine o'clock. I've got an awful lot to do and I'm getting a good bit done, thank God, but it does leave me kind of limp and no fooling. I'm writing two satirical comedies for radio, one called the "Amazing Substitute" which is finished and delivered and a sequel to it called "The Master Controller" which I am wrestling with at the moment. They are commissioned jobs so I've just got to do them and finish them by a certain date which is both good and bad for me, if you know what I mean. I enjoy doing them really. I'll let you know when to expect them on the air but I don't suppose it will be for months yet. They're being produced by Andrew Allan who used to be the CBC drama man out in Vancouver. He's quite good on comedy stuff and altogether a little brighter than average. As for *T. M.*, I have been working steadily on her of late. About three quarters of the first part is typed and in a more or less finished version. I am re-writing the last quarter and have almost finished it. It will then be typed and I shall shoot it off to you, if I may. I don't know what to think about if at all now, but I'm more interested in it than ever.

We have both read the *Horse*. I'm trying to get Betty to put down her ideas about it on paper. If I don't succeed, I'll put them down myself as well as I can in the form of a postscript to this letter. As for my own feelings about it, on the whole they have not changed. I found it the same book that we read together and the impressions of it which I formed at that time were simply re-inforced by a second reading. In other words the things about it which impressed me originally still impress me. The images which it created in my mind and which I retained all turned up in the right light on the second reading. This is by no means always the case with me. I often re-read a book and get a totally different overall impression from it, in which the values have all switched around and situations acquired new colors and tones. Clearly there are two standards in my mind when I read a book of this kind, consciously or unconsciously, I am judging it in two different ways. One, what does it say to me and to me only. Two, what does it say to people generally who give it average attention? The first is, I think by far the more important because it is more a matter of intuition and direct feeling than an exercise of intelligence. To me this book has a good deal to say. I feel that it deals with matters which are essentially interesting to me, it represents a view on life which I find significant and revelatory. It adds to my imaginative experience consistently from beginning to end and for that reason alone I place it apart from the great majority of books which come my way. To my mind the ability to reveal new aspects of people, things and events which are in themselves quite ordinary is far more important in literature than the ability to write. All of which means that I like the *Horse* for my own consumption very much indeed and there is nothing about it which I would want changed. Indeed, I would be afraid that any considerable changes would serve only to weaken the characteristic impression of the book without creating any other impression of new value. As a matter of fact I don't see how it could be tinkered with at all or that tinkering would serve any purpose. That is my own personal and spontaneous reaction—change nothing and wait for the right publisher. The book will not date.

Now as to what I think the book might mean to the average reader, that anonymous, mythical gnome who lives, presumably, in the aisles of a department store. I think that quite a section of the public would find the book slightly unexciting and yet not "restful" if you see what I mean. I find myself wondering what I would have thought on this point if I had not known that "something was going to happen." Taking the comments which you relayed to me one by one:

(A) It is written with facility but is not significant enough at the present time. This is not a criticism of the book but simply a revelation of the publisher's state of mind.

(B) The background is interesting but the story seems to us a little too melodramatic to be convincing. Since when has melodrama acquired the necessity to convince? I think what this person is trying to say is—"for a melodrama this seems to be under written." The critic here is obviously convinced that plot material of this kind can only be construed as melodrama. I don't think it is melodrama at all and I don't think our average reader would think about the point at all.

(C) It would be a better book if the last half were as good as the first. She uses many adjectives. This is beneath all notice as a comment as it doesn't even attempt to assess the book from a reader's point of view. People don't divide books up into halfs when they read nor do they think there are too many adjectives, or whether it makes the slightest difference whether a book is sketched or written. "The last scene is funny when meant to be tragic." I can see what this person means. *King Lear* is funny too but I think only to the under or over sophisticated. I don't think the general public would find the ending funny. Nor do I myself think that it is meant to be exactly tragic. To me the end is just what happened. It is the end of the story.

(E) Comments by various managers. The publisher's worst enemy is the manager in any form. This person always has to sell books and is obliged to conceal the absolute unpredictableness of the publishing business by passing superficial judgements of a pessimistic nature. All managers do this in self protection in connection with all books by new authors. It is in spite of such people that all original work gets published. The success of a publisher depends on his ability to ignore their advice consistently.

(F) "Ending magnificent but gaps in manuscript etc." If the ending is magnificent there cannot be any serious gaps in the manuscript because a magnificent ending implies a correct treatment of the story from beginning to end. (Interesting comment in view of (E)!)

(G) "Trick ending" — Fine. I don't think it is a trick ending but such endings are not usually any bar to publication. The Contrary.

Altogether, putting myself as far as I can into the "other person's" point of view, I think, the problem is to find the right publisher. I think what all these critics really wanted to say was that they found the book tedious or dull. If the manuscript of *Wuthering Heights* were sent them to-morrow by an unknown writer they would say exactly the same things about it. They do not "read" books, they "look through" them. The *Horse* certainly will never appeal to people of this kind for it must be read and it demands a certain amount of effort from the reader. I think there are an awful lot of people who are prepared to make that effort. One of the practical difficulties is that it is not possible to "type" the book and "typing" has become so integral a part of publishing that it takes a real publisher to snap out of it. Another point is that the beginning of the book is so smooth and apparently "typical" that someone looking for originality might not persist far enough to discover it. There seems to me to be two ways of tackling this latter problem — one, to re-write the first chapter or so in such a way as to reveal the originality of the book: two, to enlist the personal interest of a publisher who is prepared to really read the book. I'm afraid of the first idea [three or four words illegible] agent seems to have exactly the wrong sales technique for this kind of book, with his double identities and so on. The thing must be sold as literature and by someone who believes in it. Your present agent seems to me to have done you a bad turn with his horseplay. I would be inclined to suggest that the selling line should be this. "Here is a remarkable creative effort. It has not been written as a best seller, nor is it likely to become one but it is likely to pay its way and will add prestige to any list. It is a book that will last and may in the end achieve a considerable sale over a longish period." I think this might appeal to the smaller type of publisher who is wise enough not to be too greatly swayed by current tendencies in the business.

Betty's reaction: She read the book with great interest and at one sitting. She certainly would have done this regardless of the special circumstances. She found the domestic set-up and relations between Felicity and husband a little too uneventful in that they seemed to her to set the tone of the story a little too far down by comparison with the end. Generally she thought there was what she called—"a bit too much white nappery." She got the point of the contrast but thought it a bit too extreme for maximum effect. One specific point caught her attention. At the very end, she found the sentence "the cries of the little chickens seemed curiously loud" jarred on her and she felt that it might have been responsible for evoking a humorous idea where it was not wanted. She thought the story had a very definite appeal, with a highly individual atmosphere. She agreed with me that there should be no tinkering.

And so really there is not much to add to my original reaction. I would suggest taking the book out of the agent's hands at once. You might try sending it to some of the smaller publishers who are still interested in new writers. The big houses can now sell everything they can print on their paper quotas without the slightest effort and they are on that account a very bad market for a book of this kind. Some of the smaller publishers, although they are all benefitting by the excess of public purchasing power at the moment, are not so hard up for paper and are more likely to be interested. Their quotas of paper will not permit them to make competitive quotes for the topical "Guadalcanal Diaries" and so on and it is not easy for them to handle a best seller of any kind as they cannot print large enough editions. I would put the book forward as the work of a brand new writer and say nothing about the detective stories at all.

[One line illegible.] Things are not very eventful for us. My father is in the midst of dying in a very prolonged and painful manner which I find disturbing and depressing. It takes me quite a while to recover after each visit to him as he is simply disappearing physically in the most horrifying way. There is no hope of recovery whatsoever and he is eighty years old but apparently this sort of thing can go on for months and months thanks to the perfection of modern medical technique. In his more lucid moments he begs to be allowed to die, but they won't let him. It's a form of torture that I have never seen at close range before and I am absolutely appalled by it. Two trained nurses watch him every moment, day and night for week after week. They literally force him to go on living, or existing in a kind of nightmare twilight between life and death. There is absolutely nothing one can do about it but it is hard to forget.

I do wish you were coming east sometime, although I know you are well off where you are. How are other books, plans and the woods and the inlet and so forth? It is cold here, round about zero, but no snow as yet and the skaters are having a fiesta on a nearby river in a perfect Breughel setting. B [Betty] is going to New York on Jan 10th as her show opens there on the 11th and she has to put in an appearance for the press and so on. About forty new paintings, two years' work, will be shown. We are not at all optimistic about the show as no one is buying modern pictures and the best we can hope for is a succès d'estime. She is very lucky in having a dealer with a good gallery who is really interested in her work and does not mind whether it sells or not. He is a Viennese who had galleries in Vienna and Paris as well as the New York place. He's the only man in the picture racket whom I have met who isn't completely revolting. I think it's even worse than publishing in that the social side of it all is so deadly sickening.

I hope to send you a big slice of *T. M.* before long but I don't suppose I'll get much accomplished until after Christmas. With a child in the house and the holidays starting the end of this week things are going to be far from tranquil.

Our love to you both and please write about everything,

yours,
Gerald

23

Dollarton, B.C.
January 3, 1944

Dear Gerald—

Thank you, oh thank you for your letter! The only reason you haven't had a reply long before this is because both Malc and I have had very nearly simultaneous bouts with the flu which just laid us both out. I'm over it now and feeling O. K. again but poor old Malc is still in bed and running a temperature, though thank heavens he's finally on the mend.

First of all I'm eternally grateful to you for sending me such a long report, when I know how busy you are. But the thing that really bucks me up is your opinion on it. I knew you liked it when we read it together last spring, but after all the discouragements we've had with the darn thing I began to wonder somewhat if the final complete version would still stand up, and to say that I'm relieved that you still like it would be more than an understatement. You know the state of mind one gets in: maybe it isn't so good after all? maybe one should re-write it completely? maybe some changes here and there of things that were criticized? etc. etc. In my heart I believed in it and didn't want to alter it, didn't, in fact, see how I *could* alter it. Not that I think it's perfect or anything like that but simply that my conception of it had been so clear from start to finish that its very shortcomings seemed necessary and part of it. And so I'm going to take your advice and let it stand or fall as it is. And I'm also going to take your advice, which is also Malc's advice, and take it out of the hands of my agent, whom I agree with you is doing more harm than good in the way he's trying to market it—that is as nearly as I can tell he is, but I haven't heard a word from him since last July despite all my impassioned appeals. He just sends me these rejection slips every so often and that's all I know about it. Your advice re trying some of the smaller publishers I think is good too and I shall follow it. May I ask if you had any particular one or ones in mind? Duell, Sloan and Pearce, for instance, or Random House? Or are these not small. Or, if once small are they now bloated? Malc suggests Viking Press—perhaps Dial Press??? Or, my gosh, why don't I write to Scribner's and find out what goes on there? It seems reasonable to me that if they bought one book of mine they ought to be at least interested to *read* another one. Anyhow I'm writing Hal [Harold Matson] to-day to send it back to me and when I get it I'll decide what to do about it. Meantime you may as well keep the copy you have until I disentangle myself from my agent and then I might ask you to send it on to someone if it wouldn't be any more trouble than just sending it on back here. Will you please thank Betty for me too for reading it and sending on her opinion, which naturally I value greatly and I was so glad to know that she too agreed it shouldn't be changed. Will you tell her, too, that I know just what she means by the relations between Felicity and husband being too uneventful. I considered some counterplot there a good many times, but in the end I found the darn book wouldn't let me do anything but what I did, it's just one of its more obvious faults that to save my soul I couldn't do anything about. So all I can say is once more, thank you! The Lowrys were verging on the slough of despond when your letter arrived but now we're all bucked up and full of ideas.

Meantime your Isle of Man folder has arrived and we are enchanted with it. Where on earth did you find such a museum piece? We hope you had a fine Christmas and that all was merry with you indeed over the holidays. Ours were somewhat curtailed by the flu and the fact that Malc is still on the wagon but we staggered through triumphantly into the New Year just the same.

We keep looking out for *T. M.*??? How soon does she arrive? We look forward very much to seeing her in her final version. And what about the "Branches"? We re-read what we have lately, found them improved if possible, some of them great, but cannot know yet how to judge the whole thing. Let us know about the final status of this. Malc is still hammering away at the *Volcano,* which gets better and better all the time, I am thinking about another mystery story but haven't yet got down to it but have resolved to get started on it this month. I wish we could come east and see you (or you could come west and see us) and certainly wish we could be in New York for Betty's show. All the very best of luck to her!

The news of your father is so perfectly appalling to me I find I can't say much about it except that I know how you feel, having had a vaguely similar time with my own father. That sort of thing, that part of the medical profession's ethics, seem to me, in the light of world events etc., to be the most diabolical form of hypocrisy yet devised by man to delude himself.

Do let us know when your programs come on, you know we'll be interested to hear them, but mainly we are watching for *T. M.* There is no other news with us: the sea-gull, the heron, the seal, the whale,—all are in good form, the inlet and islands are still as extravagantly beautiful as the first day we arrived here, there are still fallen logs in the woods, and we think of the White Man more often than you would believe.

Our very best love to you all and Happy New Year—

Margie

—please do not forget to rebebber it would bake be bost happy any tibe you think of it to help place your poebs I have some ideas.

Balcolb

24

Dollarton etc.
February etc. [1944]

Dear old Gerald:

Margie just went to town for a hairdo; I sit drinking coffee looking into a green sunrise with a howling gale from the north blowing an eagle a mile high down wind; gulls & wild ducks going the other way are caught in the teeth of it and a tern gives it up, is suddenly whirled a league to windward, considers joining the eagle. How the heagles fly in great circles. Nature is the most beautiful thing I ever saw in my life. Then a gibbous moon, waning, oddly comes up over Barnet, accompanied by Venus, burning; mystical and mad seascape. Eliot says—I just read in *Axel's Castle*—"I confess my inability to understand the following stanza from Shelley's 'Skylark': 'Keen as are the arrows / Of that silver sphere / Whose intense lamp narrows / In the white dawn clear / Until we hardly see, who feel that it is there.' For the first time perhaps," Eliot

says, "in verse of such eminence, sound exists without sense." Old fool!
Too busy creaking around ruins (Margie said) the night before to know it
was Venus as the morning star. It must be admitted however that some of
his ruins are better than some of Shelley. Thanks most awfully writing
Margie at such length about the *Horse*: it really is a frightfully good
book—we were cheered up no end, and now everything seems taking a
turn for the better with Duell, Sloan & Pearce enthusiastic & almost publishing it and others interested. Some notes on Conrad, Joseph; & second
thinkings. I having sailed right through him recently. First a bit destructive. The first long chapter of *The Nigger* is absolutely the greatest thing
of its kind in literature; but the rest falls off; he might compel a landsman
to take it for granted but it is not right, & doesn't even stand up with a
much cruder but somehow more human thing like *Dauber*. No one could
find their way around that ship, he seems to have forgotten they are
rounding the Cape of Good Hope too; the very end is a horrible mixture
of sentimentality & veiled contempt for humanity coming strictly out of
the quarter deck. I think it's a failure on the whole, in spite of bits. I feel
that perhaps *Typhoon* ought to have been *The Nigger*: in spite of the fact
that it's an unparalleled typhoon, I somehow wanted it to go on longer;
which I never should have thought I would. For as he says himself the
worst of the typhoon comes at the end. This is true of the story too. The
end seems a bit feeble, & he obviously didn't like it much himself, for
here he informs us carelessly that all the while it was Christmas Eve,
which as any sailor would tell you must have produced at the beginning
quite different moral obliquities among the largely English crew. The
first time old MacWhirr feels "I shouldn't like to lose her" or something, it is moving: the second time hokum. It's wonderful in the engine
room: not so good in the stokehold. Of course it seems inevitable he
would have all the firemen passed out & the second engineer &
donkeyman doing the work; it isn't quite right just the same. That watch
couldn't have been relieved it is true, but there would have been at least
two stokers and a trimmer down there, one of whom surely would have
hung on. And if not, where were they? Captain MacWhirr is based I
think—believe it or not—partly on Captain Cook. I suppose it is still one
of the best stories one would read in a lifetime. I love *The Shadow Line*
still & *The Secret Sharer*; though *Freya of the Seven Isles* is another disappointment. On the other hand *The Secret Agent* is a surprise, an absolutely marvellous book. There is a cab drive I might mention that is
like nothing on earth had not Hugh Walpole or somebody anticipated
one. But yet another surprise is a thing I'd never heard of, a short novel
called *The Point of Honor* (or, I think, *The Duel*). If you have not read
this you must do so. Dealing with a period of history that usually bores

me, the Napoleonic wars, it is nevertheless Conrad at his very best; he has been reading Flaubert or someone & the effect is astonishing & profound. It is also frightfully funny, which I never should have thought of Conrad. Let us see *Teresina*. Let us see "Branches." We watch the post. Let us see you. Let us see you both. God bless you. God bless Betty. God bless Nick. And now the sun, terrific, a sign!

love from us both — Margie sends —
Malcolm

25

Tuesday, the 15th [February 1944]

Dear Gerald:

Well, here we go round the prickly pear: I wrote to my agent, telling him to send the *Horse* back to me, etc. and in due time received from him a long and apologetic communication which only made me feel more than ever like K. "Due to certain auxiliary circumstances," I appear to have had another cryptic message from the *Castle*. I won't go into the convolutions and involutions of the fantastic affair with Scribner's over my mystery novel: it will take care of its self in the end I dare say, but the main point was that Matson appears at last to have read the *Horse* and been sufficiently impressed with it to say that he himself was sold on its "literary merit," etc., and wanted very much to go on with it as long as there was a chance to find someone who agreed with him. He assured me that my affairs were not being neglected in the markets, even though he hadn't written me himself in some six months (he appears to have been having some troubles of his own meantime) and so, in the end, after Malcolm and I had had a serious pow-wow about it, and in view of the near impossibility of doing anything myself with the *Horse* at this distance, we decided to let him carry on for a while longer anyhow. So — When you get around to it (there's no rush) you might send the copy you have back to me. Let me thank you again for reading it and for the report you sent me on it, which just about saved my reason, as I was beginning to feel pretty despairing about it.

We have been watching hopefully for *Teresina*, will she be along soon??? I'm sure Betty's New York show was a great success, let us know about it when you write. We have kept an eye out for your programs meantime but haven't seen anything of them as yet. Meantime, despite the fact that it snowed yesterday, spring is in the air, the primroses are full of crisp new leaves, there are three tulips and a whole row of bluebells and Star of Bethlehems coming up, the pussy-willows are miaowing happily in the abandoned mill, and we gaze at Friendly Island from the pier with speculative eyes, and somehow, with spring, even hope that the White Man may be out our way again . . .

Love from both to you all! —

[Margerie]

P. S. Time, when at all, is measured here thus. This is A. D. 2, two years after the advent of the Man From the East! Am up to my neck in the *Volcano* but seem to see blue sky.

Malcolm

26

R. R. #2
Oakville, Ontario
March 28, 1944

My Dear Lowrys:

At what a long last I write! I've been infernally busy and my capacity for putting words on paper—it doesn't matter what kind they are—is, I find, strictly limited. Now, however, there seems to be a breathing space. My *News from Europe* broadcasts come to an end after thirty-three consecutive weeks. I think that's about as long as I ever want to go on with any series, in fact too long. You wouldn't think that one fifteen minute period a week would wear much upon the soul, especially that kind of a period, but it does. There are two aspects to it—first I have to read an enormous volume of very depressing material from Europe, bundles of private letters that are simply dripping with hate and despair, and then I simply have to be at the studios at 10.15 every Tuesday which in the end sets up a kind of neuroses. Tonight is the last one. I'm keeping on a weekly news commentary because it is so simple and bread earning. I don't know whether you get it out there—it is on a subsidiary CBC network that has a different outlet in Vancouver—one of the privately owned stations, I think. I've also done six half-hour radio plays since New Years. I think I told you about the three satires. They were banned at the last moment as being too too near the knuckle. I had half expected it and as they had paid for them I wasn't too sad about it, but I had to rustle up three substitutes in short order. The satires will probably be produced later, although they will be out of date if held too long. The three substitutes are nothing much, two have been produced and the third goes on Easter Sunday.

So you can see that *T. M.* has not made much progress. I had a girl typing it and she went and got married in the middle, so I don't know quite what's happened. I think I'll send you the part already typed. You've heard most of it but still I think it would help to have reactions to a more or less finished text of that part which can be perused without too much physical effort. I hope to get a good bit done on it next month when I will be rid of the broadcasts, but so often they cook up something else for me to do and I can't really afford to refuse anything reasonable. Still I hope.

Here the spring is about to make a fairly early debut. We have had very little snow this winter, so the transformation will be rapid when it comes. I suppose it has fully arrived with you by now as you were talking about flowers what seems like months ago. About the middle of next month we move back to the other house beside the water (the address remains exactly the same). We have been forced to think about next winter's quarter which seems an awful long way ahead to do things, but necessary. To rent is quite impossible so we are I think about to buy an old coach house in the town of Oakville and make it fit for habitation. It is huge and we will be able to contrive a really good studio for Betty which she has always lacked. Her show in N. Y. was, as we had anticipated, a succès d'estime but no more, strictly no more. Which made us a little sad. One always hopes for the miracle, and sure enough it doesn't happen, time after time. We are almost a little alarmed about the Aiken household as we have heard nothing from them for months and they were in very low water at the last report. Several letters from B [Betty] have drawn no response which is distinctly unusual.

I was delighted to hear that the *Horse* is being better treated. I was sure of its ultimate triumph but things can take an awful long time and it's good to know that they are moving now. And how about that *Volcano*? I feel that the recent eruption of Vesuvius should not be overlooked as an omen. I'm looking forward to the news that it is finished, that book, and to reading it.

Seems to me it was just about a year ago that I was with you, or is my reckoning at fault, a little earlier, perhaps? Anyway, it has been far too long. I nearly made Vancouver in the fall but there has been no chance since and I don't see any on the horizon. It's such a hell of a long way, but when I think it is only a day's journey by plane it seems incredibly stupid that it can't be undertaken every month or so. I don't suppose there's any chance of your coming this way. I would like to be able to think of many compelling arguments to pull you east but honestly I can't think of any, at least of none that have genuine validity. I know how well off you are beside the inlet. Still I don't give up hope that something may shift you this way, something like an urgent necessity to visit publishers in N. Y. who are clamouring to do business with both of you. That will happen of course, but why not soon? Remember that we have plenty of room and that N. Y. is two hours by plane with ten flights a day.

There have been some additions to "Branches" but I am not over pleased with them—in themselves not bad, but they don't fit into the general framework as I would like and are inclined to be concerned with side issues. If and when I send you the *T. M.* I'll send also a copy of a radio thing in which there is a song that might amuse. The music written for it in the production was poor and I think you might do much better with it in your inimitable fashion. From the radio point of view the show was very successful but the composer didn't get the point of the song at all.

I expect the picnic season will be open with you by now. I can't forget that magnificent day we walked to Deep Cove and it was so hot along the road. I wonder whether the mill is still silent there. It won't take long for the forest to reclaim the site if it stays idle. One feels that those wooden houses could be so easily re-absorbed into the general growth and so quickly lost in the fierce competition of the trees. The woods here are so utterly different. A few days ago we had an ice storm. We woke to find everything, absolutely everything coated with clear shining ice to a depth of about half an inch. All the trees had come down to earth as it were with branches sweeping the ground blocking the way in every direction. The air was filled with the sound of cracking wood as the branches were torn off by the thousands. It was acutely painful. The tops of all the white birches were the first to go. We felt that it was a catastrophe but locals tell us that it is just a kind of natural pruning that automatically removes the weaker limbs and thereby benefits the trees in the long run. The real damage is in the fruit orchards, if the trees are old and have not been kept well pruned. The sun came out and a cascade of ice particles started which went on for twenty-four hours. The noise was terrific and afterwards the ground was inches deep in ice cubes as if it were the refuse ground of some Divine refrigerator. All the wires came down and we were without electricity for hours. That's rather serious for us as everything in this house is electrically run except the fireplace. The net result is that the trees have jumped up again and we have more firewood than we need for the next year lying all through the woods and along the shore.

I'm sending some photos which may give some idea of the place in winter. I repeat that this has been a poor winter for snow but, as you will see, we get enough to give the right impression. There is none left now and the ice on the lake has nearly gone. In places it is piled up along the shore twenty and thirty feet deep in January—very fascinating with caves, grottoes and gulches that change completely over night.

Do please write and tell all, but everything, I mean, and say hello to the Islands for me,

yours,
G N

27

Dollarton, B.C.
April 24, 1944

Dear Gerald:

First of all let us say we both thought *T. M.* absolutely first rate and read it with much excitement and enjoyment and profit. We should have answered long before but the Lowry menage has had a slightly disrupting time of it lately and we weren't in the best form and we wanted to *be* in the best form when we got down to the serious business of criticism and appreciation. (Nothing serious wrong with us, just minor harassments like dentists, colds in the head, etc.) We read it separately, without discussing, and made our notes separately, so as to give you two different opinions. Possibly the most helpful thing would be to give you our notes, made while reading it, and let you see what you make of them. Remember that while we were reading with pleasure, we were doing what we do between ourselves, that is, being hypercritical and looking for everything we could find to pick on.

Margie's notes

General first impressions. First of all the real feeling for the city, that is, the city written of as though it were a character whom you knew well and loved. I think that particular thing is rare and it enchants and interests me very much. Also the people, particularly Teresina, who is swell, Roberto, and Signora Bicci, they are completely successful. I like the way the story itself unwinds and weaves backwards, and forwards. You have certainly achieved a "style," and what's even better a style that seems to grow out of the substance of the book and be part of it, and not just grafted on. That apparent simplicity is so darn hard to get. Scenes I found particularly good: in the church, in the garage, introducing Gian Giacomo, all the scenes in the Trattoria Buffo, Roberto's trip back from Naples. I find the story as a narrative always moving, sympathetic, and finally exciting.

Criticism: Very few and those toward the end. I cannot believe in the scene between the two policemen in their office, nor in the long speech of Maria Buffo's. And something in the scene at the door with T. M. and Pezzoni worries me too. I'll have something more definite on second reading or perhaps I'm wrong. I know these are essential scenes and it isn't the scene itself I object to, I think it's something in the treatment.

On Second Reading

Chap I and II I am even more impressed the second time by the parts about the city itself. It's much more than merely good description. It's like a real identification with the spirit of the city that somehow communicates itself to the reader.

III Description of garage is swell!

IV Minutiae: p. 26 line 4, there's a comma I'd delete after "but." Unusually good understanding of feminine thinking and feeling here I feel.

V I think this difficult scene is brought off with a bang.

VI And this is handled perfectly with just the touch of humor and irony to save it from being either clinical on one hand or depressing on the other.

VII This church scene is *so* good, *particularly* the bottom of p. 43 about the smell of the church. Minutiae: p. 50. after "stream of words" I wouldn't paragraph. It's confusing.

VIII Love scene in trattoria very good except "You fool," she breathed. Couldn't she just say it? This is merely personal taste.

X I like the tennis game!

XIV P. 93 minutiae: I should not paragraph after "flask of red wine" top of page. All this is such good build-up for the trip to America later and fine ironic contrast with Maria Buffo's view of it at the end.

XV This is all swell until the very end, where I find it a bit melodramatic. Not that Italians don't act like that, I'm sure they do, but can't you tone it down a bit? Suggestion: When she slams the door, instead of trying to break it down, perhaps he could act innocent and ask her why she's behaving this way? He could say he wished to talk to her about the best way of saving Roberto but if she doesn't wish to talk it over, what can he do? etc. etc. the threat would be there just the same. Then when she pleads she's too tired, he'll finally say all right and go (this saves his own face to himself too) but she can hear him quietly slipping the key from the lock.

XVI Piddling criticism due to writing detective stories: p.108, middle of page: they had clumsily placed themselves at a disadvantage. This seems dubious since you've just said it was pure luck that the Gallia found out in time they were after him, also that they've done such a careful job of searching that if he hadn't known of the police visit he'd scarcely have suspected it. So they haven't been so clumsy it would seem.

XVII Wonderful scene where Roberto sees the money in the toilet case! This whole drive back is full of suspense and excitement.

XVIII I still find myself objecting to this scene between the policemen. I can't *hear* the dialogue, it sounds like a radio script or a movie but not like people talking. Of course I know it's stylized. Possibly the fascist secret police do talk like that but it's bad art I can't help thinking. Perhaps the solution would be to have as much as possible of the dialogue in oratio obliqua. Maybe let's see out of the window: does one see the Pantheon? Is it surrounded by new buildings? What about the street below, and the sounds. I'd like more about Rome.

XIX Final speech of Maria Buffo. I'm afraid on second reading this still worries me. I know it's stylized but I still feel it's somehow too *pat*. Perhaps it merely needs breaking up in a few places. The paragraph preceding it, that begins "And Teresina wondered whether she should pray" etc., is particularly good. But perhaps if the long speech itself were broken in one or two places, by, say, letting us look at Maria, her face on the pillow, the noises of the trams outside, something like that. Or perhaps even if it were prefaced by some sentence that told us that Maria had been lying there thinking all this out (I know that's obvious yet somehow it isn't, quite) or that this is the gist of what she said during the long hot afternoon, speaking from time to time. I see that this speech is essential to the book as a whole and has its place, but I do feel that as it is I can't somehow quite believe in it and I find myself willy-nilly wondering if thoughts of political freedom would occur to a dying woman of her type. They seem more fitted to a man. Particularly as it seems Maria herself has not suffered particularly from the Fascists. I foresee the mechanical necessity of having the Trattoria sold so T. M. and Roberto will have the cash to make their escape and I believe in the reasons Maria gives for making that stipulation in her will, that's a bit of good construction I admire. One thing more: Maria has known Roberto all her life. She obviously approved of Teresina's marriage with him, but she must know he is rather weak. It seems to me a mother's dying words to her daughter should contain something more personal, — "Roberto is a good boy, but you must be firm with him . . . " something like that.

Malcolm's notes

The book should push on to very grand things: Teresina herself is an enormous success throughout. The style seems to arise naturally out of the material and is in itself a real achievement; original and uninfluenced—on first reading it seemed a little monotonous but it is somehow just right—recapitulatory, doubling back on itself, its final effect is poetical and the perfect medium for the unfolding of the story, which afterwards you are scarcely aware has not been proceeding straight ahead, so buried was the author's touch that, so to speak, "fled and pursued transverse the resonant fugue."

Piddling criticisms; and genuflections.

8. Do not like the dots or asterisks; nothing will persuade me they are not a weakness. So suggest you begin Chap II with They drank the real soft wines etc. which is better musically, too.

13. Type error: Poussin.

14. Beautiful and subtle description here.

20-21. Admirable echoing stuff in the garage. Giacomo done excellently.

24. Very piddling criticism: a slight feeling of too many gots and gets, though you need got rather drunk. *Note* Teresina, Roberto, Signora Bicci, all unqualified successes.

Chap VII Beautifully done! Likewise Chap VIII.

60. Type error: instinctively. Enrico Pezzoni is introduced brilliantly. The tennis game is a delight, and I'm very glad you used it. The drive to-

ward Naples after the game is particularly good; and everything proceeds with excellent architectonic balance and swing; no criticism here—it's fine.

101. But I have a criticism of your handling of the Enrico Pezzoni scene; I feel you want a little more subtlety. One feels a little dubious about the key business; on second reading you see it is probably O. K. after all, but a doubt sticks. The propositioning seems a little bit too true to type, and that it probably would be, doesn't seem to help artistically. At first I wrote: One solution to it might be to cut (top of 100) "If we can hit on some arrangement suitable to everyone concerned," keeping the rest of Pezzoni's sentence in. Keep all Teresina's thoughts as they are, and the key incident as it is, only when you get to Enrico threatening her outside, at the very bottom of 102, take what seems to be a curse off the passage by saying something like: She could hear every word he said. Pezzoni had drunk heavily at dinner, and he was threatening them both now. Then "what he and the others *could* do" rather than *would*. Now I feel this is a pretty lousy suggestion, but still it may suggest something to you. Or it might help if you said there, or earlier, something of this nature: There seems, in all Italians of Enrico Pezzoni's stamp, some inner compulsion to behave at given moments like Baron Scarpia in Giacomo Puccini's *Tosca*.

But the last words of the close of this chapter XV are really beautiful and moving. 104. All the business in the Continental excellent and exciting. 108. But I am not sure technique is right at bottom (see later) and I object to the asterisks. Better change chapter. Roberto's drive becomes wildly exciting.

"I hope that Roberto does what I told him ... that and nothing more."—"This may be the chance you're waiting for, Roberto," happily as they balance each other, seem slightly what one might call "cartoon technique"—I think that such complete simplicity can indeed come off: but here it started up at me. I do not see what would be wrong with: And he almost persuaded himself ducking under the shower that everything else would be easy, so long as Roberto did what he was told, and nothing more.

And: In fact it was perhaps the chance he'd been waiting for, he thought as he reached into his pocket for the door-key. Or at any rate just one of them in monologue. The rest is splendid.

122. passim: I do not agree with Margie's criticism of this though perhaps it would be a good idea to see something out of the window—per-

haps a Roman movie house or something, with what is showing there
—and a few more of your pet trams, the Monte Sacro one far from home?
—if this impossible at any rate a brief sense of Rome again, striking the
chord of the opening chapter. The best of literature is like Flash Gordon
at times, as this must be here, unavoidably, if you are to keep it simple. I
think, however, you could take any curse of that, or of possibly too
blatant radio technique off it by opening Chap XVIII as follows: à la
Dostoevsky.

It is a fact, however, that the following scene took place:— Dino
Maccari, etc. . . .

130. All this is then fine until we come to Maria's last speech, which I
question.

This too struck me as very fine when I first read it, but on second
thoughts perhaps it is a little too fine. Certainly you need something of
the kind thematically, and its ironic contrast with the brothel owner's
ideas of America is very great; though you don't get this immediately.
I'm not sure that it is right aesthetically; on the other hand it might seem
quite different in the light of the whole book. Quite apart from this I
don't think Maria would *say* all of it; that doesn't necessarily matter and
perhaps it's due to my ignorance of Italians and of the country anyway. I
think one good answer to the problem might be along these lines: have
Maria make her dying speech all right, but not quite so strong on liberty,
though there must be the wish, of course, that Teresina should leave, etc.
Then have Signora Bicci carry the burden of the thematic business; after
all we have been aware from Chapter I of Signora Bicci and the Fascists
and what she feels in regard to them, and we also know her much better
than we do Maria. One becomes very fond of Signora Bicci; almost anything you want to make her say will be O. K. with the reader. But I admit
I would have none of this criticism myself. I would tell me to go to hell
here. But let a doubt stick because of our mutual reaction to the scene;
perhaps a slight cut in Maria's speech would do the trick . . . Altogether a
swell job, Gerald, a beautiful story, beautifully and originally told, and
we are all impatience to see the end of it; a swell and I believe eminently
saleable and profitable job too. Some of our suggestions will be lousy so
chuck them out. You know what you need for the book as a whole;
whereas in spite of your having told us the general broad outline—so that
we know to some extent what you're building towards—we still of necessity can't see it all and therefore may make some stupid criticisms
which we wouldn't make reading the whole thing.

Only further suggestions I have that may be worth considering, if not already considered:

A. Have a short scene of sea and darkness on board the ship; and possibly one of dawn too. (By the way, I can't forget that Joe Venuti—whose record *Ragging the Scale* you used in *Storm Over Asia* once—was born in mid-Atlantic. Somehow that man's violin makes the freest most joyous and liberty sounding music of anything I ever heard except a lark. I can't help thinking that Venuti records say something about an Italian's dreams of America; I feel somewhere later, very tiny, Joe Venuti's violin might be heard off stage, furious and nostalgic . . .)

B. Have the wheel come full circle at the end, with a vision or panorama of Rome again, if only in someone's imagination, with the Monte Sacro tram, etc., as before.

Thank you very much also for the radio script, the *Pillars of Hercules* which was very amusing, and also really touching; did you send it to us to use as a model if and when we might want to try to write some radio scripts; if so thank you very much again; if not, and you want it back will you please say so? We would like so much to have heard it or hear it. You didn't tell us times or name of your Easter play and we couldn't find out when it was; we turned the radio off and on all day but with no luck.

We wish you could be here—and please come soon. The spring is not so good right at the moment and the black nights are Eridanus from pole to pole. But pretty soon bright days will be arriving again, we hope, with the White Man.

Have you read a novel *The Lost Weekend* by one Charles Jackson, a radioman from New York? It is perhaps not a very fine novel but admirably about a drunkard and hangovers and alcoholic wards as they have never been done (save by me of course) it struck a somewhat shrewd psychic blow that has rendered it discouraging to work on such for some weeks. But one plods on hopefully—I'd like to know what you thought however, if it has seriously undercut my delowryiums.

All the very best to Betty and Nick,

Love,
Malcolm & Margie

P.S. We were just about to mail this when Percy told us he heard you broadcasting from Frisco last night with William Winter, that you've just come back from England again! We are mailing this to Ontario, hoping though that you have to stop over at Vancouver and will have time to see us!! Many happy returns of a day.

28

R. R. #2
Oakville, Ontario
May 5, 1944

Dear Lowrys:—

Many, many thanks for the bumper letter and all your help. Really I've been working so much in a vacuum as far as *T. M.* has been concerned that to get two opinions all at once is almost overpowering. Needless to say I have devoured every line of the letter and I have by now I think managed to digest it all. I'd like to say at once that not one of your several criticisms was without its echo in my own mind. I have not been happy about the scene between Pezzoni and T. at the door of her flat and I'm afraid that I still don't know quite what to do with that. I don't feel that it is out of character as far as P. is concerned but it doesn't read right and after all it was Corine (my combined word for Corneille and Racine, those stern twins in judgement who were so much better at explaining drama than writing it) who said—"il faut qu'un drame soit vrai, mais le vrai n'est pas toujours vraisemblable." I have the same sort of thoughts about the scene between Pezzoni and Maccari (XVIII). The dialogue is of course very stylized and I don't think there's a great deal wrong with it as such. I have tried to convey what is to me the essential unreality of such characters. I think your suggestion to bring in a few outside bits and break the chain of dialogue fairly frequently may do the trick. I'm reasonably sure it will.

Maria's final speech is a stinker. It just doesn't belong I guess. Anyway I'm sure it will have to be completely re-written but I don't want to do it until I have finished the whole of the first part of the story. It's chiefly a matter of correct perspective I think and I can't get it yet. Incidentally I have now a first draft right to the end and I have set myself to finish it by the end of this month. Be sure that I will inflict the balance of the opus on you the moment it is finished. There will be a final revision after that of course but I'd like to have your ideas on the thing as whole before I make the final changes. God how long it is to actually finish a book. I can't understand what it is that makes it so hard. I write millions of words for radio always to a deadline and it doesn't seem so difficult.

Partly I suppose because one instinctively feels the impermanence of radio as a medium and the fact that time is the essence of the contract. I'm doing a serial adaptation at the moment of Stevenson's *The Wrong Box*—just fun—a crazy victorian romp that has a rather agreeable flavour nowadays—hansom cabs, bodies concealed in grand pianos and so on. Apart from such we've been busy. We've moved back to our house by the water for the summer and at the same time we've been involved in buying a permanent place of residence. It is now practically in the bag, a nice old tumble down frame house in the little town of Niagara-on-the-Lake, at the mouth of the Niagara River where it enters the Lake Ontario. The town used to be the capital of Upper Canada and was called Newark. Somehow it reminds me of Winchelsea, perhaps because of the square grid plan and the frame houses. Our house is near the river and looks across the water to Fort Niagara on the U. S. side. It's about ten miles from the falls. In summer there is a regular boat service across the Lake to Toronto which is very handy and the least disagreeable kind of travel. The town is now a complete backwater and has no importance whatsoever which explains why we have been able to find a house at a price within our range. Housing is desperate in these parts and we've moved about such a lot that we're dying to get into some place of our own and stay there. The final papers have yet to be signed but there seems to be no major snag in view.

You say nothing about the Saga of the *Horse* in yours. I wonder very much how it is getting on with the publishers. Of course you would have told me if anything startling had happened, still I hope for some good news there and I expect it too. Funny you should have mentioned the *Lost Weekend* book. I read a review somewhere and thought of getting it. Then three or four different people spoke to me about it in something like glowing terms. It is much in demand at the library so I haven't read it yet, but I will. I am about to set off on a slight bout of travel but not your way unfortunately. I'm going east to Montreal and Ottawa only—a purely bread and butter excursion which I would like to get out of but no soap, it has to be. Betty's mother is about to arrive here for a stay of unknown duration. She has been in a sanatorium with a mysterious ailment called neurasthenia all winter. Nobody seems to know just what is wrong with her but I guess we'll soon find out.

It's very warm all of a sudden with a hot wind blowing in from the southwest that smells as if it had come from the Gulf of Mexico. Under its influence the trees and flowers are simply leaping in bloom. We have masses of trilliums, most astounding plants. They appear in a few hours from the bare ground and at first look like pink asparagus, a few hours more and they spread out just like umbrellas. They come up with their leaves already formed and furled around the stem. In a day or two they cover the ground with large green leaves—fascinating. The flowers which come later, you probably know them, are shaped like an old fashioned gramophone horn, white blue, and bluish pink. It's funny I have quite convinced myself that these things are trilliums but perhaps they're not. They may be May Apples. We did not see this stage of development last year and it's more than possible that I've got them mixed. Only the flowers will tell.

I do hope you're both clear of the seasonal ills of all kinds. Betty and Nick have both had brief bouts of a kind of spring fever with temperatures all over the place, but so far I have escaped.

It must be really summery with you by now I suppose. I wonder whether you bathe yet. Here one feels like it but the water is terribly cold and will remain so until July. In fact it never really warms up. Send us your news, all of it, or if you haven't got any make it up, just so as you write. Many, many thanks friends,

yours,
Gerald

PART II

June 1944 to June 1945

LETTERS 29-41

June 1944 to September 1944

The Lowrys' idyllic waterfront existence ended when they awoke on the morning of June 7, 1944 to find their cabin on fire. They lost most of their belongings, including manuscripts such as Lowry's "In Ballast to the White Sea," but fortunately, as Lowry indicated in his telegram to Noxon (see 32, below), they managed to save *Under the Volcano* and other of their own and the Noxons' work.

The Lowrys—Lowry himself having been injured in the fire—were taken in by their friends at Dollarton until Lowry could contact Noxon about the catastrophe and ask him if he could raise enough cash to bring them to Oakville. "Fortunately," as Noxon recalled in his 1961 radio reminiscence, "at the time I had some spare money around and I sent him enough to get himself and Margerie east to our place on the train and they duly arrived in what was a pretty appalling condition" (Noxon, 1961).

In early September the Noxons moved from Oakville to Niagara-on-the-Lake, where they had purchased the historic "Kirby House"; the Lowrys followed them there on October 1, 1944. For the first two weeks of October the Lowrys lived with the Noxons in Niagara-on-the-Lake; then they moved into a house they had rented just around the corner, where they stayed until their return to British Columbia in early February 1945. In his 1961 broadcast, Noxon described vividly the Lowrys' arrival in Oakville in July 1944, and some of the events of the months that followed:

Malcolm was suffering from very severe burns on his back where a blazing log had fallen on him as he had left the cabin trying to rescue the manuscripts. He had received treatment for this, but it was a number of weeks before he really became calm enough—he was extremely agitated as a result of all this—because one has to understand that his world was one of extraordinary superstition. Everything that happened was a portent, and a fearful one usually. There were at the back of his mind visions of the most appalling nature and the symbolism of this fire which had destroyed their very attractive little cabin—he felt that this was much more than a small fire. Incidentally, those shacks along the inlet—they were always burning down—it was almost to be expected; they were constructed in such a way that if a flue from a stove got a little bit too hot or something, a fire was virtually inevitable. So, there was nothing extraordinary about that from most people's point of view, but for Malcolm this was really not only a disaster but a portentous happening which he would never be able to completely recover from, he felt.

In addition, at this time, by another unfortunate coincidence, just when Malcolm had started to work again on the *Volcano*—(He was now doing entirely revision work. The book was virtually completed. In fact, if he had said "it is finished"—this was in the summer of 1944—if he had said "that's it now," if we could have made him say it, I would have been perfectly happy to see it go to the publisher. But he still had things that he wanted to do in connection with it and so there was no gainsaying him.) However, as I say, he had just begun to recover from his physical condition and to get into a better sort of mental shape, able to work, when one day I happened to be . . . in the news department at the CBC on Jarvis Street in Toronto, and I heard that a Norwegian journalist by the name—or a writer by the name of Nordahl Grieg had been killed while acting as an observer in a British bomber over Berlin. He had made the trip simply in order to be able to write about the experience, and the plane had been shot down: he was killed. For some reason, I had not known up to this time of the influence that this Nordahl Grieg had had on Malcolm in Malcolm's early years. Either he had not told me about this or if he had told me I had not connected that Nordahl Grieg with the one whose death had just been announced and it was really by the purest chance that I happened to mention this. This fell like a thunderbolt and this was another of this terrible concatenation of events which to Malcolm was starting to spell out doom. So it really set him back to where he was before—really nothing more unfortunate could have happened just at that time—and it began to look as if the *Volcano* again might never see completion. (Noxon, 1961)

29

CANADIAN PACIFIC TELEGRAPHS
TORONTO ONT
JUNE 18TH 1944

GERALD NOXON R R NO 2 OAKVILLE ONT.
YOUR WIRE TO MRS MALCOLM LOWRY CARE DOLLARTON
PO DOLLARTON BC HAS NOT YET BEEN DELIVERED THIS
PARTY UNKNOWN TO DOLLARTON PO. NOTICE MAILED.
CANADIAN PACIFIC
TELEGRAPHS

30

CANADIAN PACIFIC TELEGRAPHS
TORONTO ONT
JUNE 19/44

GERALD NOXON
R R NO 2 OAKVILLE ONT
FURTHER REGARDING YOUR WIRE JUNE 18TH TO MRS MAL-
COLM LOWRY CARE DOLLARTON PO DOLLARTON BC WE
ARE NOW ADVISED AT 7 42PM JUNE 19TH THAT WIRE HAS
NOW BEEN DELIVERED OK
CANADIAN PACIFIC
TELEGRAPHS

31

R. R. #2
Oakville, Ontario
June 19, 1944

The Manager
The Bank of Montreal
Oakville, Ont.

Dear Mr. Reid:
 I want to telegraph some money to Vancouver and I would ordinarily
have arranged the matter through my bank in Toronto, Bank of Montreal,
King and Yonge Branch.

Unfortunately I'm laid up in bed to-day and will not be able to tend to the matter myself. As it is very urgent, perhaps you could arrange it for me.

I want to telegraph the sum of two hundred dollars to Malcolm Lowry, c/o Bank of Montreal, Vancouver Hotel Branch, Vancouver. I enclose a cheque on my account at the King and Yonge branch for two hundred dollars made out in favour of the Bank of Montreal. My wife who will bring you this note will pay cost of telegraphic draft, etc. in cash. I trust that you may be able to arrange this for me speedily,

Yours truly,
Gerald Noxon

32

[Dollarton, B.C.]
[June or July 1944]

Betty & Gerald Noxon.
Delighted excited journeying youward tourist arriving Oakville eight thirty a.m. Monday Margie unhurt myself fit though back fried no stiff upper lips or Nordic glooms saved Branches Detectives Volcano Purgatorio Noxon photos also Betty's picture while thousand pages Paradiso lost will reimburse gently you are saints please do not dread.

Malcolm

33

[Oakville, Ontario]
[early September 1944]

Dear folks:
    —phantom ping pong balls, an unaccounted for bicycle that rushes through the forest, & a broken sailing ship that sails eternally through a sea of green grass. A newspaper that, strangely, delivers itself.

We think of your pictures.

I broke down toward the end and produced some Blue Top for Hill the Mover in his last throes (while with heroic abnegation still reserving 4 bottles for Margerie & I to drink when she came back, at which time they were all largely consumed by myself)—explained you would have done, of course, had the beer been, as it were, yours: but knew I should not have done, as I saw Hill the Mover moving inexorably straight through the forest—none of this nonsense about roads:—"Boy, you're speaking my language!" the driver, who hailed from Vancouver, said as I was producing it and I suspected at that time how fluently that language would be spoken by the time H the M reached Niagara . . .

We think of Cleo.

Working *very* hard here. *Volcano* seems actually almost finished. We had an earthquake. We hear finally about house in N-on-the-L [Niagara-on-the-Lake] to-day, & if all O. K., we will stuff all our triumphs horrors and angels into our bags, strap them up tight, and so be seeing you again soon; we will arrive in a barrel, at least bring one; but for the Yulations, & certain memories of one Capt. Webb.

We swim in the lake which is still very fine indeed—the heck with those bacteria boys; can't you see them, on the Caribbean, say, on holiday: "Although marvellous weather we were forced to spend most of our time in the stuffy cabin down below because of the tons of coloric bacteria (wrongly called spray) being flung to leeward up on deck."—A gull visited us, but on being disturbed, crashed straight down through the bushes into the lake, & sank for a while, so full of pickerel he couldn't clear the trees, presumably . . . I had a contretemps with the chinless wonder in the bank, the asst. mgr., who discovered himself insulted, Gerald, because he hadn't been introduced to you. I thought of saying to him that that was because he was only the asst. mgr. He managed however to be quite offensive which makes me think there must be something about me which arouses antagonism: don't I know who have to shave every 3 days. We owe you money, will re-pay—also Nick.—Thanks a million for everything: sorry, I was probably a loathsome guest, a sloth or mud lark might have been better. But I myself am marvellously bene-fited: as also Margie: can only hope I didn't spoil your summer too much. Mushrooms of fabulous size & destructive appearance have sprung up each morning & ourselves with them, discovering they are edible; delicious, though we have not yet tried Destroying Angel bor-delaise! My mother has sent me *The British Weekly* which contains News of the Churches, Across Asia Minor in an Araba by Annie C. Burt, Kirby Ferguson's columns and an article on the Robomb, "By this we mean that we must not be satisfied with arrangements & precautions such as the punctuation of our sky with interfering objects. We must beat it at its own game . . . in a fair field . . . from the very outset. We modestly but firmly believe that this can be done. Our conviction rests finally upon what might even be called a theological prejudice or conviction." God bless—love to Nick.

Malc

34

[Oakville, Ontario]
Sunday [September 3, 1944]

Dear Gerald:

Well we've more or less settled down to work in more or less peace and quiet, though the house seems very queer indeed without you all and we haven't got used to it yet.

We've been gorging ourselves on your tomatoes and corn and believe it or not have had two more very succulent meals from your green beans. And this morning I gathered nearly a basket full of walnuts lying along the drive which no one seemed to be bothering about except the squirrels and the worms. They're as yet very green of course but doubtless will ripen.

Yesterday in the post (by the way, I hope you've received your mail by now which we've re-directed to you at Niagara-on-the-Lake) a letter came from Mr. Wilson saying that the first script was officially O. K.'d and for me to go ahead on the others, which I shall do shortly. You still have the copy we kept of the first one and it would help me greatly to have that by me as I struggle with the others. So if it isn't too much trouble could you send it along? And what happened to the library book, *Nine Tailors*, wasn't it?

I haven't yet had the note from Miss Ball about the house so I think I'll drop her a note. I don't know what the snag can be if any, surely the Rent Board or whatever wouldn't insist she should charge *more* than she wanted to. However...

Tell Nick we haven't forgotten his $5.00 and the only reason it is not enclosed is this: we went to the bank yesterday to cash a cheque and the assistant manager came bustling up and put us through a very irritating five minutes. He said *he'd* never met us, that you'd only endorsed one cheque for us and then cleared out, etc. etc. We were furious and have determined not to go near the bloody place again. As soon as we hear definitely and finally about the house I'm going to cash in our tickets and we'll just live on that money until the move if we starve!

Best love to you and Betty and Nick from us both,

Margie

35

Niagara-on-the-Lake
September 6, 1944

Dear Malc and Margie: —

Thanks for letters. Horrible about the Bank, especially after we'd gone
to the trouble of fixing things there as we thought. I'm just about to dash
for the boat to town but I will put this with the *Nine Tailors* and the script
and post the lot when I get to Toronto. We are up to our eyes of course,
but there has been some progress, thank god and we have an electric
stove in. We've both been feeling kind of groggy after the move but are
gradually recovering. Please let me know if you don't hear from Ball
about your house. I think there may be other possibilities here, now that
the Vicar has called. Yes, he really has and of course he knows all about
us. Ontario is a very small place in spite of its size.

Yours hastily,
Gerald

36

c/o Noxon
Wynwind
Judge Snider's Estate
Rural Route No. 2
Oakville, Ontario
[September 1944]

My dear Gerald and Betty:

The house, without the Red Dragon, and the Silver Flagon; and all, is
emptier of itself, and its beauty, somewhat like a body from which the
spirit has fled: the body I am thinking of I saw, one late December, in a
[Cruz Roja] in the Palace of Cortes: it lay there, whole and uninjured, in
its feet, and a small boy jumped over it gaily, twice, in and out of its
arms, to get to the phone while the doctor thumped it on its chest, once,
as if greeting a boon companion. Its owner was not there, it seemed, but
still alive and gay somewhere, perhaps gone to have a drink.

It is a very gay carcase too, to wrap ourselves in which we are endlessly grateful (I also wrap myself up sometimes in the cold abandoned
oilskin of Justice, when Mrs. Young is not looking, and go out looking
for toadstools in the rain) never more so than late last night after returning from Toronto whitherto, in order to re-establish our awareness of

reality, we had made an enormous pilgrimage to see—what but *Pelleas and Melisande?*

You do not think that is funny? But that is very funny. That's so, gentlemans.

For perhaps one way of re-establishing one's awareness of reality is not to go to Toronto on a Friday night which, although beautiful, is not unlike Liverpool on a Sunday night, and listen, in the middle of a dark wood, in the Massey Hall, in Shuter Street, to Debussy's whole tone harmonies, expressing such words as:

GOLAUD
Pourquoi avez-vous l'air si étonnée?
MELISANDE
Vous êtes un géant
GOLAUD
Je suis un homme comme les autres . . .
MELISANDE
Pourquoi êtes-vous venu ici?
GOLAUD
Je n'en sais rien moi-même. Je chassais dans la forêt.
Je poursuivais un sanglier. Je me suis trompé de chemin.
—Vous avez l'air très jeune. Quel âge avez-vous?
MELISANDE
Je commence à avoir froid . . .
or		MELISANDE
Oh! do not touch me . . .
GOLAUD
Do not cry out . . . I will not touch you. But come with me.
The night is very dark and very cold. Come with me.
MELISANDE
Where are you going?
GOLAUD
I do not know . . . I am lost also.

Toronto frightened me, my first experience of a city since Vancouver; the pubs were shut, we took a Flash Gordon experiment to the Royal York Hotel & found a catacomb: the gigantic chained doors of a Bastille informed us, in a kind of underground Piccadilly Circus of the soul, that the ladies beverage room was closed: Margie had to escort me, gibbering, across the street, where we were unable to purchase a chocolate soda.

In all this darkness the supramodern twinkling of Brights Wines in Yonge Street gleamed brightly; shut too, however.

I was shaved by my barber who after four weeks is still humming *Moonlight and Roses,* now in whole tone harmonies: "Everything must have its opposite, light dark, good bad: now take some of these old civilisations, some of these statues these old ducks put up, the Egyptians or were they the Chinese, I dunno, these statues there, in the desert: their enemy is deterioration: yes, deterioration: they say the noses of some of them old ducks fell off, of these statues there, in the desert, I dunno . . . Ha ha! May I ask you one thing: you are not a Catholic? Then I tell you something — moonlight and roses — This war — moonlight and roses — is a war between the Catholics and the Protestants. The Catholics is the bad; sir, I dunno. Perhaps you would know?"

I have met too, having a hot dog, the Mad Fisherman of Oakville. He says he was not a friend of Captain Webb's. His proudest boast is that he built the barrel with his own hands in which his friend Bobby Leach went over Niagara Falls three times. The barrel was made of steel hoops with red plush inside. Later Bobby Leach slipped on an orange peel in Niagara and died at three o'clock in the morning in the Station Hotel, with the Mad Fisherman by his side. He is a great man, I think.

The lake this morning is radiant molten cobalt to the horizon and flowing fast in every direction; there is an endless white Alaskan mountain range of clouds, above which is a blue sky, and below which the coast line is clear, with Niagara Falls an approaching train.

The other day we turned left toward the railway and found ourselves in fields of flowers and butterflies up to our necks, seven different kinds of daisies, purple wild asters, goldenrod, wild primroses, milk weed blowing, and locusts and dandelion colored butterflies (so that it was like walking in a lilliputian airport) lilac mushrooms and, on the horizon, under the trees, a single blue green white horse, stamping . . .

The day was blue and hot, the railway lines ran into mirage at both ends, and the firemen of the trains were practising *Mood Indigo* on the Wurlitzer organ or perhaps it was the Golaud theme from *Pelleas.*

We are doing well on our works and eating your corn and peppers and your wonderful tomatoes (and they say there is not immortality!) — and even beans.

—*Teresina* has a front seat here, however, and we are reading same with renewed enthusiasm. I think also of the Inspector of Signs. What a wonderful opportunity you have to do a more than Dead Souls of England here!

There was a very strange noise outside last night and the Asst. Bank

Manager has grovelled before us on his nose in the ante-room of the Halton—drunk as a lark!

The lease has arrived and we are very excited.

>							Best love to Nick and you both,
>							from
>							Malc

P.S. Margie will have written you re arrival etc.: your hospitality is deeply appreciated: hope we will not be too much trouble, Betty,—certainly we are in much better fettle!

P.P.S. Extract, Betty, from this Indenture.

... M. Lowry, hereinafter called the Lessee of the Second Part, Witnesseth that in Consideration of the Rents Covenants & Agreements respectively reserved and contained on the part of the said Lessee, his executors, administrators & assigns to be respectively paid observed & performed the said Lessor has demised & leased and by these presents doth demise & lease with the said Lessee, his executors, administrators & assigns, all that messuage or tenement situate lying and being in the town of Niagara, County of Lincoln, & Province of Ontario, composed of Lot Number Twenty-five (25), known as the Misses WINTERBOTTOM lot...

37

[Household Notes from Margerie Lowry to Malcolm Lowry]

every morning on arising

open door at bottom of stove—open draft on chimney
fill tea kettle 2/3 full from *hot* water hydrant
remove front left-hand stove lid—
place kettle over fire
Take your salts—using water from hot water taps
look at living room stove—(open drafts if it looks
unhappy, & put sprinkle of coal on [Malcolm's parenthetical instructions])
measure coffee into coffee pot
when water is boiling in kettle, pour into top of
coffee pot
wait 5 min.—call Margie

between 10 & 11 every day

empty ashes in stoves
shake stoves down until fire falls
fill with coal (*note* consult Margie about kitchen stove on account
of cooking but always fill other)

4-5 everyday

fill 4 coal buckets
Monday night   —garbage
Tuesday   "   —*ashes*
Wednesday "   —garbage
Friday   "   —garbage

between 10-11 EVERY night

shake down *both* stoves until fire falls
fill with coal
be sure drafts are closed on both stoves
top door (damper) on living room stove *slightly* open

38

[Oakville, Ontario]
Saturday [September 1944]

Dear Noxons:

    We've heard about the house and all is O. K., so unless something really drastic, and I can't imagine what it would be, occurs, we'll be seeing you on the first! Meantime, if it isn't too much of an imposition and in your spare time sometime, could you see about the coal situation? You can only have one ton at a time put in but can order the other and have it on hand. The coal man knows them. Shall we send you a check for the coal and how much??? For some reason I shall feel more secure when I know the coal is sort of thereabout . . . That's fine about the electric stove, but how about your furnace??? Possibly it's the chilly weather that has me in this groove. I should think you would be groggy and hope you'll be sufficiently settled in when we arrive we won't be too great a nuisance . . . Wish I could have stayed and helped, Betty, I felt like a dog leaving you with all that confusion. Thanks for the stuff, I'm starting to-day to struggle with the broadcasts ... Your miraculous beans have given us yet another meal ... Malcolm wants to walk over to Niagara when we leave here, being in an adventurous mood to-day; well, *maybe* ... Madam Young corralled me for tea the other day and wouldn't take no. My God! The whole lot of the females were there ... Help! Our love to the vicar. And yourselves and Nick ...

Margie

39

[Oakville, Ontario]
Wednesday [September 1944]

Dear Gerald:

Here it [radio script] is, formally O. K., I hope, more or less, but a little gutless at the joints. Perhaps you could give it a good swift shot of adrenalin, without which dramatically, as you see, it may fall a little flat. For all I know some of the conversation, for instance, between Dave and Ronny re mathematics etc., just lacks plain verisimilitude and it may be that there is slang here and there of the kind to which they would take ex-ception. However I hope nothing much remains to be done and that it won't put you to too much trouble. I have worked hard on it, especially upon the narrator's features which were extremely difficult, I found, to fix at the requisite low level but I hope that these are clear euphonious and suitably moronic. It's also a little difficult since I've practically never listened to any radio plays, etc., and also, handicapped as I am by lack of even the most primitive education, to write convincingly on edu-cational subjects. Well, anyway, here it is and I'll be awaiting your judgement and advice and perhaps this isn't too bad for a first attempt in a new medium.

We're both fine and working hard, no news from this end, hope you and Betty and Nick are settling down and recovering by now. No time for more, the postman is approaching and I want to get this off to-day. Love from both to all,

Margie

I haven't any copy of this, so please return with corrections. Many thanks.

40

P. O. Box II
Niagara-on-the-Lake
Thursday [September 1944]

Dear Margie:—

I'm sending the script back to you at once. It seems to me absolutely O. K. and I have no suggestions worth bothering about. I saw Wilson yesterday and told him it was all under control. So just send it to him, and I suppose Beattie will get a copy too. The script may be a trifle long but there is no point in worrying about that now as I can see a point where it can be cut quite simply if necessary. It seems to me you have picked up the style in very short order and the others shouldn't give much trouble. Wilson approached me about some more work when I saw him but we can let that wait until the present assignment is finished. You may not want to be bothered with it, but there's plenty to be done this winter if you feel inclined.

I ordered your coal long ago 4 tons. It can be delivered whenever you like. There doesn't seem to be any difficulty about deliveries here so I thought you would rather wait until just before you move in. Any way your order has been on the books for over two weeks so you are quite O. K.

I'm writing a special program for V/day which is involving a hellish amount of work in addition to the usual two a week so poor *T. M.* has taken a back seat. Progress on the house is notable for its complete absence, but we are getting used to the sense of thwart and are just pegging away at it. B [Betty] has been to town—great event and has bought some wine colored corduroy for curtains—all our best to you both,

yours,
G

41

[Oakville, Ontario]
Saturday [September 23, 1944]

Dear Gerald:

Herewith the next broadcast. I hope it's as good as the last one but still feel so unsure of myself in this new medium I can't seem to judge it. I was delighted to say the least, and, quite honestly, very much surprised that you hadn't any changes to make in the last one. In fact, paralysed.

Not that I hadn't done my best with it, of course I had, but considering my absolutely abysmal ignorance on everything to do with the style, medium, subject, etc. etc. I can't help feeling it's just a fluke. Still—one's sense of dramatic values must come to the rescue unconsciously: that's the only way I can explain it. Anyhow, here's another, somewhat shorter. Perhaps too short???? How many pages exactly should they be anyhow?... What do you mean I won't want to be bothered with any more work from Wilson, for gosh sake, how else are we to pay the rent, not to mention the coal bill, this winter? Don't let it get away. I read that news with much relief and glee. And thank you, thank you for ordering the coal... Re the next broadcast after this one, could you send me a booklet of Mr. Beattie's which he gave me called "Looking Ahead" and which he suggested I use in solving Ronny's interview with the Counsellor.

Well, a week from to-morrow is the first and we are thinking it may be better if we left here on Saturday the 30th. I've studied your train schedule left behind and seem to find a train leaving here as of about 2:06 P. M. which would presumably get us into St. Catharines around 4 something and which would be a good one it seems to me, but I'll check on this further and let you know definitely, if this is O. K. with you. The lease has arrived for the house, and we can move in on the 15th so will only be quartered on your hospitality two weeks: hope this isn't too much of a bore for you and too much trouble for Betty. Have written to Dollarton, etc., for some winter clothes and had them sent to Niagara c/o you, they may arrive before we do so some day when you're at the P. O. you might just mention it so they won't be sent back.

A most mysterious thing: the other night Malcolm found, in a wicker chair in the living room, a small blue leather change purse containing $15 in bills, $1.71 in change, 3 tickets on the Hamilton street car lines, a key made by Beck, Hamilton, a sales claims slip on one Birk's (no address) dated July 9 (no year) and one (1) Eaton's inter-store coach-service good-for-one-fare bus (I suppose) ticket. Does this belong to you or Betty, or do you know of anyone who lost such a purse in your house? It was in plain sight at the side of the cushion. Why didn't we see it before??? Tell Betty I made some yummies the other day without baking powder and they were swell. Much better. I have her dress from the cleaners long since and am bringing it. We are very much looking forward to seeing you all again how is Nick getting on in his new school hurray for the wine-colored corduroy we are bringing our beer rations intact the weather has been fine and the wood pile you left will last love to all from us both—

Margie

LETTERS 42-46

February 1945 to June 1945

The months the Lowrys spent in Ontario (from their arrival in Oakville in July 1944, to their departure from Niagara-on-the-Lake in February 1945) were hardly idyllic despite both Lowry and Noxon having anticipated such a visit for a long time. Lowry, drinking heavily once more, acted (as he himself put it) like a "mud lark" during these months with the Noxons, but attributed his erratic behaviour to the stress of having lost his home: "a patch of place which actually belonged to Malc, or as he told me," Noxon told Aiken, "his first home" (Noxon, 1945). In any case, Lowry was eager to return to Dollarton, and in early February he and Margerie did so, despite Noxon's protestations that they should stay in Ontario, at least for the winter, where he could find work for them at the CBC. Of course, Noxon well realized (as he wrote Aiken right after the Lowrys' departure) that Lowry was struggling to come to grips with the meaning of the Dollarton fire and the loss of the manuscripts, and that Lowry "had come to the conclusion that he could not accept this blow from the Gods without fighting back" (Noxon, 1945). Noxon saw that before Lowry could go on with other work, "[h]e had to go back there and re-build the shack and re-establish his corner of the Paradiso" (Noxon, 1945).

At Dollarton, after assessing the situation, the Lowrys resolved to build on their old site even though "strangers and vultures" with "rackety, rickety children" (Lowry, p.49) had moved in and were building a house right alongside. In late spring the Lowrys moved into their still unfinished cabin—where they were now to come increasingly under the threat of eviction by local authorities—and Margerie again began typing *Under the Volcano*. In early June Lowry—"after taking some thought" (Lowry, p.45) and without a word to Noxon—sent the manuscript off to Harold Matson.

42

Dollarton, B.C.
February 7, 1945

Betty dear—
    Raining like Niagara Falls ever since we arrived—stayed 2 days with
Whitey—have rented the house we first had 4 years ago—stove falling
apart, no towels, pans, or wood, Malc has a majestic cold, somebody has
started to build right where our bedroom was & Malc is wild! But here
we are & it all looks as beautiful as ever in spite of everything & will be
squared away in a few days. Meantime we miss you like anything. The
daffodils & bluebells are coming up in our old garden. A miracle! Love
to all from us both.

Margerie

43

Front Street
Niagara-on-the-Lake
Ontario
February 23, 1945

Dear Margie & Malc:
    I was glad to find your card reporting a safe arrival in B.C. when I got
back from a trip to the Maritimes. I was away for over a week, travelling
all the time and feeling pretty exhausted at the end. Nick was in bed for a
fortnight with what the doctor (little Rigg) called bronchial pneumonia. I
think it was what used to be called simply bronchitis but he was pretty
sick and B [Betty] passed an irksome time at the bedside. He seems O.
K. again now.
    The snow is still with us although it has been thawing fast now for two
or three days. The great drifts are shrinking but at this rate it will take a
couple of weeks to get rid of it all. Various forgotten horrors are starting
to emerge in the yard behind the house and of course there are ashes
everywhere. We have had the furnace men for many days—the cellar is
now practically solid with pipes but they are by no means finished and
are plotting the upheaval of the whole kitchen floor on the next visit.
However the system is now working almost as planned and funnily
enough they switched it on for the first time on the warmest day of the
winter with the thermometer at 50. It has been pretty warm ever since and
I think the completion of the job will definitely mean the beginning of

spring. So be it. There will be no complaints about spring when it does arrive. We have had quite enough of this spectacular winter.

Incidentally I read about the colossal rains in your part of the world and wondered if Dollarton was badly flooded. I thought it improbable owing to the lie of the land. And yet—well, it only needed a flood to round off your experiences with the elements.

B's show of water colors is now on at Eaton's in Toronto—no reports of further sales yet, but I am fairly hopeful. When I was in Montreal recently I fixed up another show for her there to follow this one, a mixture of oils and water colors. Some of the new pictures are very exciting. I finally got around to building the easel for B that I have been promising for years. I put the greatest care into the job particularly in order to get it to stand solidly. Of course it wobbles all over the place because it is accurately level on the bottom but the floors are not. So I must think again. We have painted the wood work in the front hall and in my work room—white, it takes many coats to cover the horrible brown but my, what a difference.

Now, about "Moby Dick," I think, if a second episode is finished, it would be a good idea to send it to Andrew Allan at Canadian Broadcasting Corporation, 354 Jarvis Street, Toronto, Ont. (The offices have been moved from York Street.) Send a covering letter with it saying that you understood from me that he (Allan) was going to do something with it and that you had therefore gone on with the work and that you would like to know if he has anything more definite in mind in connection with its production. I think it would be in order to ask him if he could let you have some advance on it. As I told you, he knows the circumstances and I think he will do whatever he can for you. In any case I think it's time that you got into direct contact with him about it. As he will certainly be out on the coast during the summer it will be possible for him to contact you later about the production and I think it would be an excellent thing for you to meet him.

I keep pretty busy churning out dramas for the two series which Andrew has running at the moment, mostly pretty corny. And I have started on the second part of *T. M.* Incidentally I have not had the slightest acknowledgement from Quincy Howe of Simon & Schuster in connection with the manuscript, but after your various experiences with Scribner's I am not in the least surprised and have simply written the whole thing off in my mind. After all it's only a matter of three weeks or so and who am I to expect a letter inside of a year. I feel like a man who is just starting to climb an immensely high mountain of solid ice. With my tiny hatchet, which has incidentally a soft rubber handle, I have succeeded in scratching out a single step after years of work. And above me

I see countless other minute figures all busy scratching away at the hard, shiny surface. At the summit sits a man in an easy chair doing a crossword puzzle. He is very bored and wonders why no one ever comes to see him.

Well, anyway, I expect the flowers and things are coming out for you and I do hope that Malc is getting enough quietude to press on with the *Volcano*. Please write, tell all and above all your prospects for rebuilding.

Yours with love,
Gerald

P.S. How did the pirate trunk survive the ordeal?

44

April 3 [1945]

Dear Betty—
Please forgive, etc., my long overdue reply, etc., and report on the Lowrys. We have, as you may well guess, been on a merry go round since arriving. But first of all a heart-felt thank you for the chicken, without which we should most certainly have starved en route: the train was ancient, the dining car *fantastically* ancient and ill equipped and everyone stood in line all day long from one meal time to the next to get in at all. The train was full of soldiers and sailors and the trip was long and tedious. We ate your tarts and munched your almonds and devoured your chicken and believe it or not the little valise was emptied just before arriving. And in this department, a loud word of thanks for the beautiful tin box which it must have cost you a pang to part with and which I use constantly to keep cookies etc. and which is indispensable in this damp place as you can imagine. And of course I have nothing of the sort left. Thank you for relaying the cable, Malc replied and we have heard nothing further and so far all goes on as usual in that department. And all the final and obvious thanks which are none the less heartfelt for all your help and thoughtfulness—oh hell, you know what I mean to say!

I'm so sorry to hear poor little Nick had a spell, that bronchial pneumonia stuff is NO fun, I remember having it myself when I was about Nick's age, please give him our love and hope he's out in the beautiful spring weather I see by the paper you're having. Note of irony department: we're having heavy frosts, it snowed twice day before yesterday, and weather has been generally perfectly foul.

News here is jumbled and mixed. On the good side of the ledger we are typing the *Volcano* and are more than half finished. It will be very fine to get it in the mail at long last, which I hope will be accomplished before April runs too far into May. Also we have, actually, the platform for our house nearly finished. And what do you know? My proofs arrived when we had been here a week or so. Curious, isn't it, that I should have to come back to this very house where I began to write it in order to get the proofs? We're living, in case I didn't mention it, in a tiny place we rented when we first came to Dollarton, about a quarter of a mile down the beach from our house. We used to walk by it and think how our past lay here—just as well we didn't know the future lay here as well, eh? Well, anyhow, the proofs arrived, the first half in duplicate, one copy carefully corrected by a proof reader and then re-corrected by Mr. Weber. I added my remarks and returned them and a little later arrived the second half of the book. This time only one set, uncorrected by anybody. I waited for the corrected set, in order to O. K. any stupid corrections they may have put in, but they never arrived so I think poor my book is going to press (if it hasn't already) without my seeing what they've done to the last half at all. Oh well... funnily enough, I don't give a darn. I daresay it'll be all right and anyhow the truth is I don't care.

News on the rather more debit side: Malc and I both had ferocious colds no sooner had we arrived. He was stricken first, in the middle of trying to drag baggage down the hill, get in a new stove in the house we'd finally managed to rent after bunking with Whitey for a few days, etc. Then it hit me and I had it for six weeks before I could throw it off. In bed and out again, up and down, cough and sneeze, blimey! Meantime it rained and rained and RAINED. And is still raining. The most calamitous blow was to find some perfectly frightful people (whose faces look like uncooked biscuits) building a horrible, high, enormous, hideous, house sticking right out so far it cuts off the sun and view, over where our bedroom used to be. And this despite our pathetic notices left all over the place, evidence of the burnt house, and even after they were told we were coming back. We pleaded, argued, tried to bribe, all to no avail. They have squatted; and every day from our window we watch their house rising higher and higher and becoming more and more horrible while ours remains as yet in the realm of hopes. Lumber is almost impossible to get, but we've found a chap from whom we can purchase when we have the wherewithall some two-by-fours at not TOO bad a price, some second hand ship-lap for walls, etc., and some fine second hand windows all at a reasonable price, considering what prices are these days when you'd think everything was diamond-studded. Whitey has

helped us build the platform,—he had been saving posts for us all winter
whenever they drifted in and so had Sam—but now he has to get busy on
his own work preparing his boat for the summer fishing trip to Alaska.
So now we'll have to do it ourselves, or try and hire someone, not much
hope, but never give up, don't fire till you see the whites of their eyes
Gridley, I have only begun to fight, etc. etc. And we haven't had a sign
of life nor a word from Allan, despite having written him twice (once before Gerald's letter and once after) so as you may guess by now we are
practically flat broke, and so stuck, so far as starting building. But
there's plenty we can do in the way of cleaning out the burnt places and
trying to rebuild the steps, prop up our beloved pier, and so we work here
on Malcolm's book every morning, rising at 6 o'clock, and go up there at
noon and work until exhaustion sets in, then we come back here, eat, and
fall into bed. Meantime, we can't buy any wood so we're in the forest
cutting our own and trying to dry it out and believe it or not, we're having fun and seem to thrive on the hard life. Malcolm is in fine form, very
happy to be back and full of pep and cheer, he says to tell Gerald he's
started a letter in reply to his seven times so far and will finish it soon,
but every time he gets five minutes and starts in again I send him off to
the store, or to saw some more wood, or go to the spring after water, or
we have another frightful storm and he has to get the boat up the
beach—or, well, you know how it goes. But he sends his best love to all
and a letter will be on its way any day now. I'm enclosing a plan of the
old house and the new which Gerald will be able to decipher and you'll
be able to imagine what we're doing better than as if I tried to describe it.
So—best love from Lowrys to Noxons—spring is on the way and God
bless you every one—

Margie

P.S. I kept your P. O. M. O. till the other day intending to return same
but feeling very broke I finally weakened & cashed it. Forgive stupid letter—I love you all!

45

Dollarton P. O.
Dollarton, B.C.
May 14, 1945

Dear Gerald & Betty—

I must apologize for not having written long ago but what with this &
that, I haven't had much time, or my hands have been covered with mud,

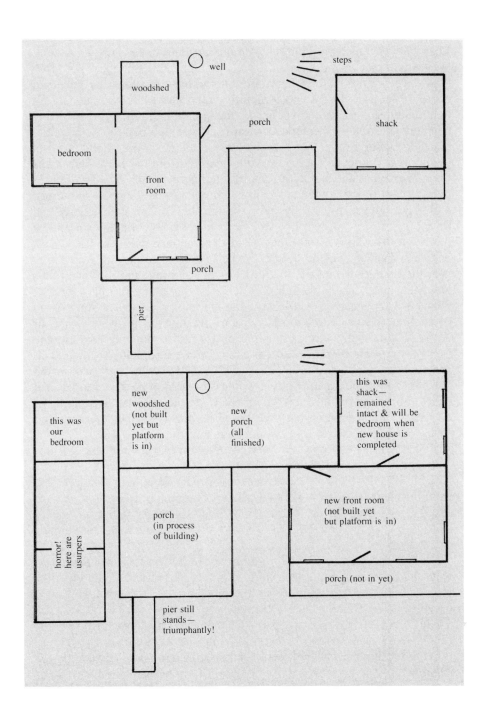

or there was a creosote post we needed drifting out to sea, or we were finishing the benighted *Volcano* —we still are, really are, this time:
Margie's just finishing typing the tenth chapter—or, we had an accident.
We had, in fact, a bad accident—precisely the same thing you did, Betty—Margie ran a nail in her foot, but with near disastrous results. I
couldn't get a doctor (it was a Saturday afternoon) to come out, or, for
that matter, contact one to get her to; the situation didn't seem to warrant
hospitals & stretcher bearers, it wasn't, at first, too painful, so we first-
aided it ourselves, feeling the chances of tetanus were slight: we had
overlooked blood poisoning, & the next morning that was what she
found herself with; result, hospital, a temperature of 105, and an extremely foul time for Margie. All this a month ago—she came out a fortnight ago, but can still hardly walk, though she's very much better & will
be about sprightly as ever in a week or so: it was the first day we got the
lumber for the house (we already had the foundations in) so work on it
has been held up, & the lumber—when last looked at—was still lying
near the Dollarton wharf with all its innocent-looking nails in it. All this
has been pretty grim, though we contrived some fun out of it here &
there, & I have become, at least, what we least expected, a pretty good
cook. Margie was under morphia a lot of the time when I went to see her
at the hospital—the way there being past a movie showing Lon Chaney
Jr. in *Calling Dr Death,* a funeral parlor, and a Fire Station—in a semi-
private room with an old lady of 94 who had broken her hip, also under
morphia, in the next bed. Margie would say, over & over again, "Blank
pages, millions of blank pages," to which the old lady would reply "Oh,
oh, what should I do is that you Ada 3 bedposts is 4 I'm stuck now."
"No, blank pages," Margie would say, and the poor old lady: "What
shall I do, I'm done up, I'm done up, Peg are you there? I've got this
wolf and I've pulled it down . . . Who has come in downstairs—Oh, it's
hard, it's hard—Alas for those sweeps—is Mr. Way there? I jumped up
from the chair & I tried to get to the bathroom—I jumped up from the—"
"Not at all! Blank pages! Millions of blank pages!" "Oh gran you've
wet the bed again,—what's that my garter? your doctor? No, my garter.
Your daughter—? No no, my garter." "Blank pages, that's what!"
"Give me the scissors please, to-morrow I'll be washing and shaving. I
want the scissors to cut it off to-day. Who are those four? Come in, come
in . . . I can see you. But I can't see who you are. What happened
downstairs?" "Blank pages!" "I know you're there, but I can't see you.
There was such a noise, a noise—what happened? It was a noise like
tin." "Only blank pages." "Stop moving that furniture! They were all
moving furniture . . . Nurse! Nurse! help! help! *The moon's coming in the
window!*" —

I'm sorry to hear about Nick's having had bronchial pneumonia, & hope that he is quite O. K. now. I expect also that you will have spring by now; if so, that is more than we have, save for the rain part of it, though the woods are very fine and lush and full of wild bleeding heart. I have begun to swim, tentatively— Margie not yet; but she probably will when her foot's better—

I hope sincerely, Betty, that the water-color show at Eaton's was a great success, as also the oils & water-colors show, later, in Montreal: you certainly *deserve* great success, by god—the Great Face behind sometimes seems to have oddly delayed plans, though, in regard to the careers of artists. If I ever make any cash myself that has not the mark of evanescence upon it one of my first actions will certainly be to buy one of your pictures. Margie's proofs arrived—the first half in two batches, one batch uncorrected by the proof reader, the other corrected; she was instructed to look out for another similar two batches, comprising the last part, but only one batch arrived, the uncorrected section: reluctant to send this back corrected by her, contrary to Weber's instructions, she has held on to it, awaiting the corrected portion, but it has still not arrived: meantime there is every reason to suppose that the book had been already sent out in some prepublication form without Margie's corrections at all: Weber once more has resumed his perplexing castellan silence, but there is cause to hope that owing to "certain auxiliary circumstances" things are looking up a bit from what they were: in fact, since Scribner's cannot bring out her second book later than November, under contract, it appears at the moment that she may have two books coming out at once. I hope, Gerald, that *T. M.* clicked with Quincy Howe—what is the news on this? If there are any initial disappointments, which I sincerely hope not, you must brush them away and get on with the second part, while they iron themselves out into encouragements. But I wouldn't have thought you'd be having much trouble in getting it placed—perhaps Simon & Schuster are bringing it out now, as I write: I hope so. Matson would be glad to handle the book, I know, if you require an agent: his address is 30 Rockefeller Plaza, New York 20, N. Y.: but then, of course, perhaps you might not be glad to handle Matson. We have no radio as yet so haven't heard you recently on the air—. I suppose you must have been pretty busy with V. E. Day: We like to hear your broadcasts, though, very much indeed (Vancouver's local efforts are not very high class)—tell us when we may hear another drama from your pen, for we may be getting a radio soon. We have listened under poor circumstances to the remaining Margie's & Margie's-&-my efforts: *Maria Chapdelaine* came through pretty well, though poorly produced, & *Grey Owl* very well, I thought. *Sunshine Sketches of a Little Town,* the one in which I had the largest hand, had the distinction of being the worst thing I've ever listened to in any medium whatsoever: however, just as you told us they wouldn't, they didn't use 1/4 of our script. I think they were quite foolish not to, since under your tutelage, the difficulties in the way had been adequately smoothed out, I thought: as it was, they achieved something really awful, and even stuffed in a gruesome joke about a drowned man turning green, as presumably more suitable for children. We were hurt since even Whitey, whose radio we were listening to, thought we must be morons for having written it. Re "Moby Dick" we are a bit bewildered and wish you could find out for us how the land lies, if at all. We have written twice to Allan but so far got no reply, in spite of the comparative urgency, several months ago, of our request for one of some sort. I suppose he has been busy with V. E. Day—or teeth troubles—still & all—dying though we are to do it, it's a bit hard to go on with a project of that kind as we'd like to do it without some kind of further say-so on the subject, as you intimated yourself: the result has been that in watching the post each day we've been discouraged from proceeding further, though it's all planned out, and with the *Volc* almost completely done, we're rarin' to go. We have had also some heartrendering moments re the house: people have built a bloody great babel on our old bedroom, they tore down our flags and our stakes, & repellent infants dance upon our pier. Nevertheless we're still building it, & by expanding on the other side, we'll have a nicer place than before eventually. We are in our right minds again, at all events, so that I see my lugubriousness as your guest in sad perspective, though it was very fine to be with you all at that & a much appreciated privilege—as also to know the unique Niagara. Well, perhaps I shall do best to cull some advice for us all from an obscure book of Melville's—"Never wait for calm water, which never was, & never will be, but dash with all your derangements at your object, leaving the rest to fortune"—Best love to Nick & yourselves from us both, as to Mrs. Lane [Betty's mother] and Mrs. Noxon—

affectionately,
Malc

46

Front Street
Niagara-on-the-Lake
Ontario
June 1, 1945

Dear Malc & Margie:
    I was relieved to get Malc's letter a few days ago and I was all set to make immediate answer when lo I was smitten down by one of those

ghoulish summer colds, a visitation too horrible to be dwelt on. I am just beginning to emerge, but the summer alas has departed. This morning I had to light the furnace! Circumstance unparalleled in local history. We have had abominable weather tricks—hell hot in March—cold in April—18 consecutive days of rain in May and now this—It honestly looks and feels like snow.

But enough of these glooms, and I hope an end to your misfortunes too—oh, those rusty nails. Nicky got a huge thorn in his foot and we have been taking him for the series of anti-tetanus shots etc. And proof-trouble—well, I don't know, it's something to see some proofs—I mean actual printed stuff on paper of what you have been writing. As for *T. M.,* I am off on the merry, ghastly jog around publishing town. So far it's been to just two—Simon & Schuster and Farrar & Rinehart—no dice at either. The physical effort of shipping it round is already too great and I think I will send it to Matson. I feel completely fatalistic about it and I feel that the inexplicable, incalculable Matson with all his utter mystery and bafflement is perhaps after all in possession of the key to the labyrinth. I think perhaps that these things are just much, much more difficult than we innocents think—on a totally different plane somehow. I happened across Thomas Wolfe's little piece on publishers in *The Web and the Rock* the other day and I relished it exceedingly. Yes, I shall send it to Matson, who will doubtless pick it up and ride off in all directions, arriving after immense toils in the exact center of no where at all.

But things go on. I have started a new opus—not the sequel to *T. M.* which can wait a while, but a story that has been long in mind. It's about a man who is very rich and builds a huge and elaborate wall surrounding nothing at all. One day he is found dead inside the wall amongst the weeds by two children. The book is all about how he came to such a place and end. Part of it is set in England and part in Toronto where the wall is. Typical incidents—(the book is called "Clegg's Wall" the guy's name being Arthur Benjamin Clegg) birth of Clegg in a private hotel in Cromer England circa 1885. Clegg shows utmost resolve not to leave the comfort of the womb. School—the young Clegg is being obliged to kiss the toe of a tough young colleague. He bites hard instead and almost severs toe. In the alarms and excursions he disappears to be found later locked in the new fangled water closet. Headmaster breaks down door to administer brutal beating. Home—thirteen year old Clegg steals novelette belonging to the housemaid. She chases him to his room to get book. A struggle ensues which suddenly takes a sexual turn in the middle. Shocked housemaid cuffs Clegg who locks himself in room. Clegg senior returns to break down door and administer punishment.

And so on—Clegg accompanies his father to Scotland for shooting.

The open country terrifies him. He is found in a distillery dead drunk. Doctor advises against Clegg being sent to Public School. He goes to private tutor in London instead. There he refuses to get up and nails the blinds down on the windows. Exile—tired of his son's eccentricities, the elder Clegg sends him to Canada where he seems to turn over a new leaf. He becomes very industrious. He lives on nothing and acquires a huge fortune in the bond business. This is made possible by the fact that he is completely unscrupulous and uses his gentlemanly appearance and speech to deceive widows and pensioners. Then he begins to build the wall. Huge boulders are hauled from the Lakeshore to the site on the outskirts of the city. A crew of Italian stonemasons spend several years building the wall. It is completed, the massive gates are locked and that is that. Clegg is tired of money making. Desperately he makes a last effort to avoid his final entry into the walled space. He tries to break out of himself, to make contact with the world. He tries priests, whores, youthful innocence, vicious old men in a series of horrible encounters. Nothing doing. Clegg was a mistake. He should never have been born. Inside the wall the weeds and undergrowth have flourished unchallenged and in the midst of this jungle Clegg shoots himself.

The book will not be very long—just a series of short episodes. I imagine it sounds rather morbid, but Clegg is actually quite cheerful in a grim way and there is a certain humor throughout.

I was talking to Andrew Allan on the phone this morning and for the umpteenth time asked him about "Moby Dick" and as usual got nothing satisfactory. But I do know that he is at present engaged in cleaning up all unfinished business re scripts before setting out on his annual holiday trip to Vancouver. I imagine therefore that you will hear something from him very shortly. He has got very much behind with things, not entirely his own fault I know. He has scripts of mine nine months old on which he has made no decision, although of course he has bought lots of others since. If you don't hear from him before the end of this month, I would suggest your contacting him when he is in Vancouver in July. I'm sure he means well but . . . it's the same old story.

We hope that the re-building has been making progress and that Margie is again mobile,

All our best to you both and . . . keep us posted.

Yours,
Gerald

PART III

December 1945 to Spring 1952

LETTERS 47-53

December 1945 to Spring 1946

With *Under the Volcano* in the hands of Lowry's agent the Lowrys —though not without anxiety—made plans to spend the 1945-46 winter months in Mexico. They left Vancouver in late November, stopping briefly on their flight in Los Angeles to visit Margerie's family. As Douglas Day has described in his biography of Lowry, the trip to Mexico badly unsettled Lowry; the series of coincidental encounters with people and places from his first visit in 1936-38—many of whom had found their way into *Under the Volcano*—made it seem as if, in an eerie way, Lowry was beginning to live the Consul's story. Once again he sought comfort in alcohol, usually mescal. To compound Lowry's feelings of uneasiness, Jonathan Cape now asked him to consider undertaking yet again major revisions to *Under the Volcano*.

A stunned Lowry—undoubtedly recalling Noxon's expressions of firm belief in the greatness of *Under the Volcano* as it stood—wrote the now well-known appeal to Cape (see his letter of January 2, 1946 in *Selected Letters*) in which he justified virtually every aspect of the novel's structure and content. But he also broke down and, on January 10, tried to kill himself.

On March 8, 1946, the Lowrys left Cuernavaca for Acapulco. Lowry's worst fears were realized when he and Margerie were approached by officials from the office of Migración who accused Lowry of being in Mexico illegally, and so the Lowrys were confined to their hotel. After three weeks of appealing to the office of Migración, they were allowed to return to Cuernavaca. No sooner had they done so than they received word that both Jonathan Cape and the American publishing house of Reynal and Hitchcock had accepted *Under the Volcano* without requiring extensive revisions. Lowry's joy at the news was tempered by the Mexican government's announcement that as writers (as the Lowrys had identified themselves on their Tourist Cards) he and Margerie presumably were "working" and therefore violating Mexican law. On May 4 the Lowrys were deported from Mexico.

Although the Lowrys had hoped to spend a few days with the Noxons in Niagara-on-the-Lake, and in April had, indeed, cabled their intention to Noxon, the ordeal and humiliation of deportation left them exhausted and longing for the peaceful seclusion of their cabin, and so they returned to Dollarton.

47

[Mexico]
[December 1945]

Mr. & Mrs. Gerald & Nick Noxon,
   ... of an overloaded style; we just dropped in here on the way—where? Feliz Ano Nuevo Y Feliz Navidad—we think of last year—Best wishes for *T. M.* & Works address: Wells Fargo, Mexico City, Mexico, D. F.

Malc & Margie

48

Front Street
Niagara-on-the-Lake
Ontario
January 18, 1946

My dear old Malc
   How I wonder where you are. Your compass which points neither to the North nor the East, nor the South nor the West, but always upwards has led you where? I don't know but I do care. Knowledge being lacking I must fall back on instinct to know where you may be—the mechanics of it I ignore absolutely, but you are clearly, from supernatural evidence received, in Mexico. Bene. A portent—Mexico D.F. and I thought you in B.C. D.F. or B.C. What matter? They are all just letters of the universal alphabet. But I am nevertheless almighty concerned about what has happened to your book. The *Volcano.* I am concerned (A) because of you (B) because of it, because of the value of it, because it is a great book,

and a major piece of writing. And because I know very well that amongst the books of our time it will endure. It is not so much that I am concerned about it being published, although certainly I wish it would be, but that it should be finished, completed, signed sealed and delivered as a work. A work that has grown out of much anguish which I know, much that I do not know, but all that is of importance to me, in that I believe that what happens to one man, happens to all. Queer, that the writing of a book like that is something which should help everyone everywhere always as *Tom Jones* does and *Pilgrim's Progress* and *King Lear* and God knows how many others. Many, but not so many that one can ignore a new one. Really Malc I do think, that if by any chance you haven't sealed the *Volc* and sent it off to someone, you should and pronto. But probably you have and all this is wasted and nonsensical, but knowing what the book is and feeling about it as I do, (I have been re-reading) I am more than ever convinced of its greatness and that is in no ordinary terms but meant in all and complete conviction and judgement. And I think myself capable of judging. I delayed long in writing to you properly after you left here for diverse reasons. One, I knew that only you were able to solve your problems and that what was sometimes offered as help was really only hindrance. Two, I knew that you would be living in a world far removed from mine if you were re-building your house. Then, I knew that any inattention on my part would be understood, for the very simple reason that we have always understood one another. The reason for that is hard to see, but it remains a fact and always will. Difficult, impossible and improbable you have always been, Malc, and you can repeat the same adjectives in my respect and yet, beneath or perhaps above those considerations, there has been from the first a kind of understanding that endures. I don't know where you are going or what you are doing. I have certain ideas, naturally, because I understand you. You may, I understand, be bound for a place you once knew and wish to re-visit. You may be bound for some new place that you have never seen. But wherever it is or whatever it is, remember that you have been one of the few artists that I have admired, one of the very few men that I have trusted and one of the few writers that I have read, feeling that I was in the presence of genius. And I mean "genius" in the good old fashioned sense of the word. And let me add one old thing Malc and that is a belief in the fact that you are a "good" person and that nothing you can do or accomplish or work at can have any influence on that: you will die, not as you were born, but better. A hell of a lot better than most of us. This is a letter about you. I meant it to be such. As for myself "Branches of the Night" are being published first, in periodical form here in Toronto! Of all places and eventually in book form in the same place. I am amazed but there it is. This is immensely pleasing to me because all that I have is in that writing. But how can a man live by poetry and, conversely, how can a man live without it.

Yours,
Gerald

49

CANADIAN PACIFIC TELEGRAPHS
VIA MEXTEL
CUERNAVACA MOR 14
1946 APR 15 AM 8

GERALD NOXON
PO BOX 11 NIAGARA ON THE LAKE ONT
VOLCANO ACCEPTED LONDON NEW YORK SAME DAY NEWS
RECEIVED LARUELLES TOWER HUMBOLDT 24 CUERNAVACA
MORELOS WHERE LIVING YOUR LETTER RECEIVED DEAR
FRIEND CONGRATULATIONS BRANCHES LEAVING SOON
NEW YORK HITCHOCKS [sic] EXPENSE LOVE SPEND FEW
DAYS NIAGARA BEFORE RETURNING DOLLARTON IF YOU
CAN STAND ME LOVE BETTY NICK FROM MARGIE AND
MALCOLM LOWRY

50

FRONT STREET
NIAGARA-ON-THE-LAKE
ONTARIO APRIL 16, 1946

MALCOLM LOWRY
HUMBOLDT 24, CUERNAVACA MORELOS
MEXICO
REJOICE EXCEEDINGLY WITH YOU TODAY STOP WAS NEVER
IN LEAST DOUBT ABOUT VOLCANO SUCCESS BUT VERY
GOOD TO KNOW OTHERS CONFIRM STOP NO NEED TELL YOU
BE CAREFUL MOTION PICTURE RIGHTS VERY IMPORTANT
STOP HOPE SEE YOU BOTH SOON LETTER FOLLOWS LOVE
HAPPINESS TO YOU BOTH
GERALD NOXON

51

Front Street
Niagara-on-the-Lake
Ontario
April 16, 1946

Dear Malc and Margie:

Great news indeed. I had been wondering, naturally, about the *Volc* and yourselves and where you were and what you were up to and a list of other queries as long as your arm. And I had a feeling too that when word came from you at last it would bring news of the *Volc's* completion. How strange it must seem to have finished it and how excellent to know that it will be appearing soon. I wonder whether you have made many changes? Well, I shall soon know.

And so you are in Cuernavaca. I feel I know it well, having walked its streets with Laruelle, the Consul, Hugh and Yvonne so often. And you are going back to Dollarton. Of course we'll be delighted to have you stay here on your way. Betty is at present in Washington. Her father has had a heart attack and she has gone down to take care of her mother and the house and everything. I don't know exactly when she'll be ready to come back, but the idea is that I should drive down and get her sometime before the end of this month. However I don't imagine you will be passing this way before the beginning of May if you're going to stay in N. Y. for a time. I have been down there this winter and am now writing for the Columbia Broadcasting people.

I am full of questions about the *Volcano*. Who's going to publish it? When? Was Matson handling it? Who is the mysterious HITCH OCK mentioned in your wire? (Could he be the hind legs of Reynal & Hitchcock?) Do they know—the publishers—what kind of a book they have got and will they be prepared to give it the build up it so richly deserves? And so on and so on. It is very exciting after such a long time to know that you have a truly great book and that it is going to be a huge success—every time I re-read it and I have done so often I become more enthusiastic. And what a movie it would make! There is so much to ask now that I know that you are not lost in the jungle. And quite a lot to tell.

This after receiving a letter from Betty which does not do much to elucidate matters. She doesn't know how long she will have to stay in Washington. But that doesn't matter. Just keep me informed as to your movements and I'm sure we'll be able to connect here without any trouble. When I do go to fetch her I won't be away for long and I don't suppose your schedule is cast iron. Spring is just beginning here with for-sythia and violets, but still coolish in spite of sunny days. It is one of the pleasantest times because there are few people around and yet things are waking up.

I look forward to seeing you and hearing all,

> Yours with love,
> Gerald

52

[Mexico]
[Spring 1946]

Dear old Gerald:

This is just a short note—thanks awfully for your two letters—will reply, but this is to say in a hurry that we won't be coming to New York until fall—Reynal & Hitchcock having decided that they'll publish the book as it stands if I wish without much editing—but probably it can stand a few cuts, or even more than a few, have you any sug-gestions—you know how I value your opinion—Chapter VI too long, some of the Spanish is haywire too of course—am very disappointed won't see you this summer think it would have been a good thing for Margie go New York Niagara too—I got the Jonathan Cape contract on same day after battling with them for months—they will publish it as it stands too, if I wish—Cape contract slightly contradicts Hitchcock one who want Canadian rights, so I haven't signed it yet (couldn't, for physi-cal reasons, even if I wanted to)—have had terrific battle likewise with the Mexican authorities here also that has completely worn us out, they forbade me to write another line—but what if should write to my mother in the Excusado?—And what if *we* set a trap! Grand opera but bad for us both: will write more later. British Consul virtually refused to help at all—who shall blame him? We triumphed in the end ourselves but at an awful cost both in cash & nerves. Reynal & Hitchcock apparently mean to go to town on the book however: far too much dough is already sitting in the post office here,—will sit there forever so far as I can see unless I can sign my name to it, at the moment can't, not even with a cross.

> love
> all best to Betty & Nick
> from us both
> Malcolm

53

[Mexico]
[Spring 1946]

Dear Betty & Gerald & Nick:

If we are at present a little loonier than just routine looniness there are, this time—as usual!—certain auxiliary circumstances. What with suddenly having to put up 1000 peso bond in Holy Week with all bonding companies closed or be jugged because they claimed we were working in the country—& having been held 22 days in Acapulco—Well, wait till you hear! Returning we find Malc's success all on same day while still up to our ears with Chiefs of Gardens etc. Very disappointed not to see you till fall—it seemed so good to even *think* of seeing you all again soon but R. & H. [Reynal and Hitchcock] have decided to let Malc have his every holy word & want to bring him there at publication date which is obviously better so will be seeing you then if that works out O. K. for you & jeepers! I hope it does. Congratulations Gerald on the Columbia Broadcasting & again on the "Branches." What are you doing? you don't say. Yes, Matson* was handling the *Volcano* but I'm here to tell you I know he didn't sell it, it just sold itself. Will try to write more coherently when back in Dollarton, meanwhile our dearest love to you all.

Margie

P.S. Scribner's finally published the *Shapes* can you believe it?
[Margerie]

* Advice to authors. Believe Matson O. K.: the first 150 years are the worst. He had no belief in the *Volcano* had not even read it—we both told him to go to hell then he sold it.
[Malcolm]

LETTERS 54-66

July 1946 to February 1947

Once they had returned home the Lowrys tried hard to bring to their lives some degree of normalcy. Lowry began working on the cabin again while tentatively piecing together his thoughts and notes on Mexico, which would later come to fruition in *Dark as the Grave Wherein My Friend Is Laid* and the still unpublished "La Mordida." Lowry also worked painstakingly on the galleys of *Under the Volcano*, endlessly revising them.

Their financial worries allayed for awhile, and buoyant with the anticipation of a February 1947 publication date for *Under the Volcano*, the Lowrys set out for Seattle on November 30, 1946. They made their way across the United States by bus, reaching New Orleans on December 6. After spending several days editing the page proofs for *Under the Volcano* they sailed to Haiti.

The ship reached Port-au-Prince on New Year's Eve in time for the Mardi Gras festivities. The crowds and the excitement intimidated Lowry; he began drinking heavily and experienced a series of breakdowns, each one more serious than the last. When Lowry went into what Day refers to as drunken convulsions while staying with friends in Petionville, Margerie took him to Notre Dame Hospital. From there Lowry managed to write Erskine, deliberately giving the New York editor the impression that he had been confined because of a fever and cough. In his February 11 letter to Noxon, too, Lowry blamed his stay in the hospital on his "cough." When he was released a week later—shaky but sober—the Lowrys flew to Miami and from there travelled by bus to New York, arriving in time for the public launching of *Under the Volcano*—February 19, 1947.

Stunned now by rave reviews, Lowry found the parties and promotional appearances among strangers an agony. Of their days in New York Margerie wrote with considerable understatement to the Noxons that Malcolm was "nearly paralyzed by triumph." The frenzy ended when the Lowrys departed for Niagara-on-the-Lake on March 4 to spend several days with the Noxons.

54

Dollarton, B.C.
July 29, 1946

Dear old Gerald:

Well, I guess you may have been a bit anxious about us after our odd letter from Nueva España but here we are, back in the old homestead again. Or rather, new homestead. On the whole it is beginning to look better than the old one though we are still doing a lot of carpentering. I am sitting in one of your favorite chairs and the washing is blowing on the old pier—we still sing "When Gerald comes to town" and everything in fact is as it was, only better. It is only recently we have been able to sing the said song again without mingled feelings of sadness and disaster and in a minor key but now the house and everything else is getting on so well the song is once more gay and we can even look forward once more to the visit of the White Man without agonizing over the burned posts. It is true we were nearly murdered in Mexico not long ago and in fact only just escaped with our lives across the border: but that is another story for a winter evening and una botella. Fortunately it is such a good story that all that experience now seems very much worth while to both of us. It is, however, disarming to be as it were *inside* a novel, the protagonist, or protagonists, rather than the author; but fate was such an extraordinarily good artist in this case that one forgives it for having seemed capable of stopping at nothing at all in order to gain its ends: besides, one now has been given the chance of stepping into fate's shoes for a while and writing it up oneself, as indeed one is planning to do.

News from here is all bright. Margie got so fed up with Scribner's that I have been doing her letter writing for her but to-day we got the first Scribner statement from Hal re the *Shapes* which is in the 5000 sale class and has even run into a second edition apparently, which is damn good and encouraging news albeit she is charged for corrections on proofs she never made, never, indeed, for that matter received. *The Last Twist* is coming out shortly, we hear, but not from Scribner's, via her press clipping bureau and a review in the *Retail Bookseller*: she has never seen the proofs and does not know what version they are printing. And I have high hopes of the *Horse* in England.

Reynal & Hitchcock seem to be planning to go to town on the *Volcano* and re this publishers they have proved such swell people to deal with that I do not hesitate to suggest you get in touch with them yourself, specifically with one Albert Erskine, who has in addition to the work involved maintained such a hilarious, if scholarly, correspondence on the subject that one cannot but conclude him to be a kindred spirit of a kind you would find most understanding in regard to your own works. As for Hal I would, in spite of his faults, stick to him: he shows up trumps particularly as a business agent. In the field of royalties, etc. — in short, after the event—you will find him tops: he is very slow at precipitating that event however and I would not put it past him not to read one's books at all: his judgement seems better of "writer" rather than "book." I have had to get through with the *Volcano* in somewhat of a hurry in regard to Hitchcock: I would have been better off for your advice re possible cuts etc. They gave me carte blanche and I made very few. A crashing thematic mistake in Spanish held me up for a while but I think I solved it satisfactorily. But with Cape though I have contracted to write a preface of 1000 words and also a blurb!—Can you help? I am in a considerable stew about what to say. Unlike Hitchcock, the readers of whom (all 7, as Erskine remarked) seemed to think it the berries, Cape's readers, all save 1, appeared to think the thing rather a bloody bore and wanted me to rewrite it. I refused to do this but had to battle literally for every chapter. Though I convinced them in the end there may be something in what they say, namely that the reader may be put off by the slow moving beginning unless he has some intimation of the reasons for this and the gruesomes and/or profundities in store for him and so on. I await your advice. I need scarcely add how much I thank you for your own part in and encouragement re the book. All your suggestions turned out right, and the parts you sat on, such as Chapter II, and which I re-wrote with Margie's and your help until they got your O. K. have become the strongest.

We went to—where, you seem destined not to find out since the last pages of this letter have mysteriously disappeared. However this is more or less the final bits and pieces of news etc.: Please tell us when the "Branches" are blossoming forth. The *Volc* is coming out sometime around the first of the year and Hitchcock's want me to be in N. Y. on publication date so we plan to come east somewhere round that time and are very much looking forward to stopping in Niagara and seeing you all. Our very best love to you and Betty and Nick—God bless.

love,
Malc

55

Dollarton, B.C.
October 15, 1946

Dear old Gerald:

This is a kind of interim letter soliciting some advice, suggestions, or failing that simply some moral support for one Vernon Van Sickle, a very good fellow who is by way of carrying on bravely here in Vancouver certain works bravely started by yourself in Cambridge with the Film Society, etc.

For my part I took the liberty of advising him to write you and this he is doing; as I see it his problems—apart from the usual ones of finances and the stupidity of other groups etc.—arise mainly from the difficulty of getting hold of good films, many of which are tied up, I understand, by the British Institute on the one hand, and on the other by American organizations that won't let go of them. I thought by virtue of your experience in both hemispheres you might be able to point a way of prying them loose or suggest at least some direction or possible liaison with any other group in Toronto or elsewhere that might make this easier.

So far he has done very well: *Sunrise, The Baker's Wife, Crime and Punishment, Fall of the House of Usher, The Last Laugh, Cyprus is an Island, Night Mail* and so on: and such things as *Greed, The Loves of Jeanne Ney, Joan of Arc, The Italian Straw Hat,* and *M* are being shown during the winter. He shows the silent classics for the most part at a studio on Saturday, and has the Paradise theatre on Sunday nights every fortnight, much as you had the Tivoli, for the others.

It is with the others curiously that he chiefly gets let down: he will have been promised, say, *La Bête Humaine,* but then at the last moment will be sent something dull like *Veille d'Armes* that no one would much want to see. Or *The Song of Ceylon* simply vanishes in transit.

Many films he can't get hold of at all unless he buys them outright—and this is impossible because they haven't much capital: or since it's a non-profit business, all they have goes on the various aspects of rentals. Naturally he wants to get hold of as many of the finer French modern films as he can while some of his other difficulties would seem to be due to certain films still being with the Custodians of Enemy Property. But the main difficulty would seem to be with the British Institute and the virtual impossibility of establishing any clear contact or arriving at any clear understanding with them: I feel you might know somebody there who would make dealings with them easier.

At all events I hope you will write him as this kind of work is important and can only lead to a Better Thing.

I'll reserve other news for another letter—some of it absolutely staggering—among other things, Margie's second book, of which she never received the proofs, published without a last chapter and eight months after the time limit on her contract had elapsed: I finally wrote itemizing the whole bloody business to Perkins—result: Scribner's has been turned upside down: expressions of horror, the book withdrawn and to be published again, apologies from Charles Scribner himself—the cause, unknown to the rest of the firm until now, Margie's editor there had gone mad—

All best love to Betty Nick and yourself from us both.

Malcolm

56

[Dollarton, B.C.]
[October 15, 1946]

Betty dear:

This is hardly by way of apology for my long silence since at this late date that seems rather inadequate—can you take my word for it that so damn many damn things happened that I got to the point that I couldn't write a sentence that made sense to anyone, even my mother. However, things look miraculously brighter now, one seems to be emerging from some kind of spiritual purgatory—not the least of which was our weird and nearly fatal experience in Mexico last spring. As Malc wrote Gerald, we hope and expect to be coming east this winter, to New York at publication time of Malc's *Volcano,* and are dreaming and talking every day of stopping off in Niagara to see you, probably some time in January as it looks now. If it's inconvenient for you to put us up please don't hesitate to say so and we'll bunk at the Prince of Wales or some place. In any event, you'll find a very different Malcolm and Margerie from the battered wrecks you were so wonderfully kind to before. All best love from us both to you all, and a very special heartfull to you from me.

Margerie

57

Front Street
Niagara-on-the-Lake
Ontario
October 18, 1946

Dear Lowrys:

It was very fine but more than a little shame-making to receive your letter before I had got round to writing a reply to your last. To begin with I took a month's holiday en famille which what with driving thousands of miles, staying with friends, camping in Adirondacks and so forth left literally not a second for the typewriter which I lugged with me the whole way. Then on return here I found I would have to work like a demon to make up for my time off. I should explain that radio writing is passing through the doldrums at present and one has to work hard to bring home the Spam (or Speeef, I see is the latest). This is the more galling because everything looked dandy in the spring. I had an excellent contract with CBS in New York, but the show, of which I was 1/4 author, folded after 18 weeks instead of the scheduled 52—the producer was sacked on account of his political opinions! However that disaster was merely symptomatic of and in sympathy with a general depression in radio which I think may last quite a while. The industrialists are having to pay more to labor and so have less to spend on advertising. It's a good wind but it does blow ill for some. And here in Canada the CBC has an operating deficit for the first time in its history. That puts the squeeze on programs which are always the first item to be slashed. So I have been to the grindstone, doing a lot of hack work for small return.

But enough of this stuff. The vintage has been splendid and I have forty gallons of good red wine in the cellar. I am enduring my regular fall cold, but it's becoming such a regular feature of the calendar year that I guess I wouldn't feel right if it didn't come along about now.

I'll be glad to hear from your friend Van Sickle. I'm afraid I'm completely out of touch with the film business but I do know one or two people who have all the dope on showing foreign stuff in Canada. As a matter of fact Mr. O. C. Wilson, whom Margie will certainly remember used to run a Film Society in Vancouver and was later in charge of procurement of films for the National Film Society in Ottawa. I think he still knows a hell of a lot about the game of getting good pictures which is certainly difficult and complicated.

I'm dying to hear all your various publication news and adventures. I had seen no notice of the publication of opus Margie #2 (was that the

The Last Twist or the other one?) but since Mr. X is mad he possibly kept all news of the event to himself. Really—how fantastic—no last chapter, I mean. And what of the *Horse*? I suppose you are amidst the proofs of the *Volc* or perhaps not yet? I wracked my brains about an introduction, but somehow, I couldn't convince myself of the need for one. It needs talking about, but I daresay you're over that hurdle by now anyway. Malc, how I'm looking forward to seeing that book in print. What's happened about movie rights, by the way? I think of it all the time in terms of screen values. It could make such a tremendous film. But who could make it? You must have buckets of news and most of it good, I figure. And the story of your Mexican interlude is still to be told. Perhaps you are busy writing it down?

Events with us have been few and trivial. I feel about ready to go somewhere very different for a year or so, but the practical problems are great what with school for N [Nicolas] and so on. *T. M.* continues on a weary and unproductive round and has so far evoked not a single peep of enthusiasm or even faint interest from anyone. It seems to be the perennial winner in the manuscript least likely to interest anyone competition. That is in itself a certain distinction I suppose, but not one conducive to further effort in the same direction. However I continue to scribble away on various projects with no very definite idea of completing them. At present I'm working on a short novel called "Until You Are Dead." It's got an historical background and it's about a man who was sentenced to death for treason here in Niagara over a century ago—a true story as to the main facts, but long forgotten. During the fourteen days between his sentence and the day set for execution his wife gets his sentence changed to one of transportation. He is shipped off to Van Diemens Land from which he eventually escapes to Nantucket with the help of an American whaling captain. The villain of the piece is Sir George Arthur, Governor of Upper Canada at the time and ex-Governor of the penal colony of Van Diemens Land. Sir George was a blood chilling character who gave permission to the paroled convicts in Van Diemens to hunt the native Tasmanians as they would any other game. It's a violent story and it seems to be turning out a cross between an R. L. Stevenson adventure yarn and a Kafquesque nightmare. I may send you some to read if I can ever get enough satisfactory material down on paper. I don't get a lot of time to work on it at present. "Branches" continue to grow, too, but spasmodically and not very satisfactorily.

Do let me hear all your news and everything—past, present and projected,

with love,
Gerald

58

Saint Louis, Missouri
December 6, 1946

Dear old Gerald:

Meant to post this in Wyoming, then thought (in honor of the Blues) wd do so in St. Louis, where we sit in a smoky hotel room (in the middle of a coal strike) drinking claret & eating liederkranz; our address for next 6 weeks will be Gen. Delivery, New Orleans: afterwards we hope to go to Haiti for a bit; then N. Y. (*Volc* comes out Feb.) & so home, via Canada, hoping to see *you* on way. Nothing but good news from our end. Both hard at work at new works. All fondest love to Betty Nick & yourself. —Ever.

Malc

P.S. In Wyoming we saw some live penguins; also dinosaur's bones.

59

[New Orleans]
[December 1946]

To Betty & Gerald & Nick

With best love & best wishes for a Merry Xmas—& a happy New Year—when we shall be thinking of you, as do you please think of us (we are spending ours at sea, on board a bauxite freighter the *S.S. Donald Wright,* outward bound from New Orleans to Haiti, & we are the only passengers)

from Malcolm & Margerie

Best love & every Christmas wish & hoping with all our hearts to see you on our way home our address in Haiti—
c/o Anton Kneer
Agent—Alcoa S.S. Co.
Port-au-Prince
Cheerio!

Margie

This is the second Christmas card I got for you—I wrote you all a long letter on the first one, but suddenly decided the next morning it was too

sentimental, & might put you off; more fool I—so please take the deed
for the deed

                                        Malc

                                        60

                                        Front Street
                                        Niagara-on-the-Lake
                                        Ontario
                                        January 5, 1947

Dear Malc & Margie:

Well, to think of it—you are in Haiti. We are of course bursting with
envy, particularly as, at this moment, the winter is closing in with a particularly horrid white fist. The trees of Niagara are encased in clear ice
and as they thrash about in a howling western gale, they shine under a
bright sun. At night there are loud reports as the overladen branches
come clattering down onto the frozen snow. In fact the worst ice-storm in
25 years. It's not without excitement and appeal, this winter stuff, but it
certainly accentuates the glories of a Southern clime.

And as it happens Haiti has always been one of our most cherished ob-
jectives. As you may have known, B's father was military governor of
Santo Domingo during the first world war and she spent several childhood years on the Island. She has fond memories of Port au Prince and
we've often talked of making a visit. So we are of course panting to
know what it's like. Is it the "Majorca of the New World," as *Time*
would have it? I hope not. Do please write giving us all the dope. I have a
sort of idea that once there you will stay a long time, for if it's the kind of
place we imagine it to be, there would seem to be no point in leaving it
for Canada or the U. S.

I sent an Xmas card to New Orleans, B's first attempt at a wood-cut,
for which she has no great affection, but which I rather like. I expect you
had sailed before it reached you, but maybe, in the curious ways of mail
it will find you in the end.

With us there is lamentably little to report. I sent *T. M.* to Albert
Erskine at your suggestion and I had a very nice letter from him. He
turned it down of course, but he was interested and had obviously taken
the trouble to read the book which is something, in fact a lot, judging by
my experience. He also seemed to get part of the point of the book, but
thought that it didn't quite come off.

I'm so very glad that things are going well with you both and that you
are working. I believe you said that Feb. was the publishing month for

the *Volcano* and I can tell you I shall be watching for it. Our plans continue to be rather uncertain due, as usual, to B's mother and father. They are supposed to start for Florida any day but we are doubtful as to their ability to make the move unaided, or even as to their intention to go at all. So at any moment B may be called to Washington to take charge. Sundry other consular children have been on hand there throughout the fall but they have now disappeared, one lot to Madrid, the other to Shanghai. Also B's two brothers in the Navy who were stationed in Washington are now in New England so there is no one on hand down there to cope with exigencies.

However, I hope and trust that both or one of us will be here, should you come back this way. I must say, if I were you, I would be tempted to postpone the return to the frozen North until spring has set in. But I daresay that feeling is engendered by the acute state of our winter. My car is frozen solid to the ground and I am contemplating digging it out with a BLOW-TORCH!

Our wine this year is one of the bright spots. It has turned out better than ever, dry but with a slight "petullance" that is very fetching. I wonder about the local tipples in Haiti, but on second thoughts I suppose there's everything on the no-tax basis. Still, there should be some rather special brew provided from the general background—French—Spanish —African and what not. Super-potent I should imagine with perhaps an absinthe base. You must make a report featuring food, drink, accommodation, prices etc. so that if we ever get the chance we can go there knowing what to expect. It would be wonderful to make it next winter, but just now it doesn't look much like it. The problem of Nick's schooling is not the least of the bonds that keep us stationary. Not that he learns much at school, but I was shipped and changed around so much myself and got so fed up with it that I don't like to inflict it on Nick. On the other hand I have the feeling that nothing would please him more. He carries his own world around with him in a sort of mental brief case and in ordinary matters he seems to become more scatter-brained every day. Maybe it's the age he's attained, a ripe ten now. We shall see.

What are you working at? Please let me know—and how does it go? I told you I was working on a sort of historical adventure, but that has now become nothing more than a tale within a tale, a story told on a verandah overlooking the lake by an old Canadian judge of which Judge Snider is the rough prototype—you remember, the ex-owner of our house at Oakville. The Judge himself is a character in the larger story which is called "Loretto in Titan"—Loretto being the name of a man and Titan, the name of a town. It is a strange affair and rambles dreadfully, but I'm trying to get away from the tightness of form and thought which seems to try all the time to reduce writing to a single sentence, then a single word, and in the end, silence. It seems to me that Proust, for all his annoying mannerisms, did achieve an excellent way of writing. Whenever I come back to him, I'm struck by the freedom with which he moves around in his subject, in time and space and emotion, without caring a damn for the reader and yet without being unreasonable. He will qualify some incident by referring to some minor action of a minor character 600 pages back in the book. If you understand the reference so much the better, if you don't, the passage still makes sense. In spite of those labyrinthine sentences with their conglomeration of dependent clauses, parentheses and brackets, or perhaps because of them, Proust gives the impression of saying what he wants to say, all of it, not just part of it, and he says it when and where he wants to without worrying about plot, story, characters or any of the other habitual millstones that hang about a writer's neck. As a writer he seems to me to grow while many of the things he writes about seem to have dwindled to nothing.

I enjoyed the image of you drinking claret and eating liederkranz in a St. Louis MO. hotel. Is there anything left of Basin Street? I note a jazz renaissance seems to be under way in N. Y. with many of the real old-time players being brought back from Pullman cars to trumpet as they used to in Dixieland days—also some young ones taking lessons from them, which is something. But I daresay you are listening to other and stranger rhythms where you are. B and I have been hugely excited by the works of Haitian painters. We haven't seen very much, but it has been really quite amazingly interesting. We'd be grateful for any small reproduction of local work that you could find, although I don't suppose there have been many reproductions made, probably none in color. Please write and let us know how you get on, one or other of you or preferably both. I feel that we shall meet again before so very long. We all join in sending our love.

Yours ever,
Gerald

61

[Haiti]
[February 11, 1947]

Dear old Gerald:

Thanks enormously for your newsy good letter which I won't answer now as I have been laid up in hospital with a cough & Romney's *Lady Hamilton* on the wall. We leave to-morrow & hope to be seeing you both sometime between then & now. Alas, no reproductions. But Haiti is as resplendent with artistic genius as it is filled with kindliness. Truly a miraculous place in every respect.

Best love to Betty,
yourself & Nick from
Malc

62

Murray Hill Hotel
Park Avenue
40th to 41st Streets
New York 17, N. Y.
Thursday [February 20, 1947]

Dear Gerald & Betty—

I write for Malc for he is nearly paralysed by triumph. The reviews are terrific—but we will tell you all when we see you—We shall be here about a week & are looking forward with all our hearts to seeing you—If it's inconvenient for you to have us with you we can stay at the Prince of Wales? or someplace? so we can have lots & lots of long talks & there is *much* to talk about.

We are, as you see, at the Murray Hill but may move in a day or so but wires or letters c/o Reynal & Hitchcock, 8 W. 40th St. will always reach us & we hope to see you *next week* so let us know what is feasible re transportation, via St. Catharines et cetera. Meantime we are so overwhelmed with success we are chaotic—God bless & best love from us both.

Margerie & Malcolm

63

FRONT STREET
NIAGARA-ON-THE-LAKE
ONTARIO
[FEBRUARY 1947]

MALCOLM LOWRY
CARE OF REYNAL AND HITCHCOCK
8 WEST 40TH STREET
NEW YORK CITY
COME ANYTIME BEST ROUTE TRAIN FROM PENN STATION
VIA LEHIGH VALLEY AND CANADIAN NATIONAL TO ST.

CATHARINES WHERE I WILL MEET YOU. STOP. BETTY IN WASHINGTON STOP REJOICE WITH YOU CANT WAIT TO HEAR ALL LOVE.

                              GERALD

64

                    FRONT STREET
                    NIAGARA-ON-THE-LAKE
                    ONTARIO
                    [FEBRUARY 1947]

MALCOLM LOWRY
CARE OF REYNAL AND HITCHCOCK
8 WEST 40TH STREET
NEW YORK CITY
REGRET BETTY AWAY AND NIAGARA HOUSE SHUT STOP SUGGEST WE SPEND FEW DAYS TOGETHER AT GENERAL BROCK HOTEL, NIAGARA FALLS, ONTARIO STOP SUGGEST YOU COME NIAGARA FALLS BY NIGHT TRAIN LEAVING NEW YORK EVENING OF THURSDAY FEBRUARY 27 FROM PENN STATION STOP I HAVE ARRANGED HOTEL ACCOMMODATION IN HOPES THIS WILL BE O.K. STOP IF NOT WIRE SENT TO NIAGARA-ON-LAKE WILL REACH ME STOP UNLESS I HEAR TO CONTRARY WILL BE AWAITING YOU GENERAL BROCK FRIDAY MORNING. STOP. REJOICING WITH YOU CANT WAIT TO HEAR ALL LOVE

                              GERALD

65

                    CANADIAN NATIONAL
                    TELEGRAPHS
                    NEW YORK NY 25
                    FEB 25 1947

GERALD NOXON
FONE NIAGARA ON THE LAKE ONT
DELAYED HERE PROBABLY LEAVING SUNDAY SORRY IN-
CONVENIENCE YOU WILL WIRE AGAIN EXACT DATE OF AR-
RIVAL RATHER STAY IN NIAGARA ON THE LAKE AT PRINCE

OF WALES OR SOME PLACE IF POSSIBLE SO WE CAN SEE
BETTY AND NICK WE COULD TAKE TAXI FROM NIAGARA
FALLS LOVE TO ALL FROM BOTH

> MARJORIE [sic] AND MAL-
> COLM

66

> FRONT STREET
> NIAGARA-ON-THE-LAKE
> ONTARIO
> [FEBRUARY 1947]

MALCOLM LOWRY
CARE OF REYNAL AND HITCHCOCK
8 WEST 40TH STREET
NEW YORK CITY
SUGGESTED HOTEL ONLY BECAUSE NICK WAS SICK STOP
GLAD TO SAY HE IS NOW BETTER AND ALL O.K. STOP SO
PLEASE COME TO US ANYTIME STOP WILL MEET YOUR
TRAIN NIAGARA FALLS ONTARIO WHENEVER YOU SAY
SOYEZ LES BIENVENUS.

> GERALD

LETTERS 67-76

March 1947 to August 1947

It was an exhausted Lowry who arrived at Niagara-on-the-Lake on March 4, 1947, accompanied by an equally weary, but now somewhat discouraged Margerie. After having revelled in life with an anonymous Lowry for so many years in the wilderness, she was startled to see in New York that there would be little public reward for her as the wife of a now-famous author.

During his few days in Ontario, Lowry spent what Fletcher Markle has recently called "one spectacular Monday" in a Toronto beer parlour on Jarvis Street across from the CBC buildings where Markle and Noxon often worked on radio-drama projects. There the three men laid some of the groundwork for the radio adaptation of *Under the Volcano*. Markle, who had just returned from filming with Orson Welles in California, and who was about to embark on the New York phase of his radio career, still recalls the lucidity and brightness which Lowry kept up to the end of that day as he sobered up from a weekend of brandy consumption by downing some thirty bottles of beer.

After several days with the Noxons, Lowry was again eager to return to Dollarton. On March 10 he flew ahead to British Columbia, ostensibly to prepare the cabin while Margerie, taking the opportunity to recover from the recent ordeal and to share her troubles with the Noxons alone, remained behind. Several days later she boarded a train bound for Vancouver, only to discover that Lowry had remained in the city since his arrival there, and was still busy with his drinking.

67

Edmonton, Alberta
March 16, 1947

Dear Ones—
Thank you again for all your love and understanding. God Bless!
                                love,
                                Margerie

68

Dollarton, B.C.
[March 1947]

Dear Betty and Gerald:
Home again, and very queer it seems too after all the excitement & the long trip but we are slowly shaking down & settling down to normal. (?) [sic]

I do hope, Betty, that you are still in New York & having a really good vacation & come back all stimulated & full of ideas & ambition. Did you get out to see the Constables & Turners at the Metropolitan Museum? Or don't they interest you?? I was very much excited by some of them, particularly some of the small Constables. They didn't have anything new at the Museum of Modern Art except some really extraordinary photographs but those, after all, are in another field.

Gerald, I am still haunted by "Clegg's Wall"—I hope you are working on it, if only because selfishly I am looking forward with so much excitement & interest to seeing some more—& don't forget you promised to send us bits & chapters as you finish them. Malc & I have talked about it quite a lot since we came home & both feel it is one of the most terrifyingly brilliant & extraordinary ideas we've heard of in a long time & also we feel that the actual *writing* of it is strong & clear & powerful & attacks the subject in the best possible way. M will say more in his letter which follows immediately on mine. We are absolutely determined to heckle, encourage, browbeat or whatever is needed—or not needed—until you finish it.

And I keep thinking of your home, & how essentially good & right & beautiful you have made it—& my God! how hard you must have worked to make it what it is we know! The snapshots we took all turned out very well & I'm having copies made which will be sent you as soon as I get them.

My trip was utterly without event: I slept from 9 to 9, the windows were frozen, I stared at nothing & vaguely read the mystery stories I borrowed from you—the food was foul: nothing but boiled codfish & bad chicken salad smack across the country—I am deliberately refraining from giving you Malcolm-news (it is all good, however [in this brief parenthetical insertion by Malcolm some words illegible]—Malc) as he will give you that, but we have such a swamping mess of mail it'll take us a month to catch up with it.

But the yellow primroses are blooming in the garden—very overgrown with weeds—reproaching me constantly—the wallflowers are heavy with buds, the forest has that heart-breakingly lovely misty look of first new green, the wild bleeding hearts along the path to the store are already beginning to blossom—& Whitey sends his love—

God bless you—give Nick our very best special love & a look in the Atom Bomb ring—if he is still interested—& to you both a whole heart full of love & friendship—and gratitude—from us both [these last three words added by Malcolm].

Margie & Malc

69

CANADIAN NATIONAL
TELEGRAPHS
NEW YORK NY 10 704P
APR 10 1947

MALCOLM LOWRY
FONE DOLLARTON PO DOLLARTON BC
COLUMBIA BROADCASTING WANT TO DO ONE HOUR RADIO VERSION OF VOLCANO FOR NETWORK. FLETCHER MARKLE DIRECTING SELF WRITING RADIO VERSION. THEY OFFER YOU $350.00 FOR SINGLE PERFORMANCE RIGHTS RECOMMEND YOU ACCEPT. PUBLICITY EXCELLENT FOR BOOK SALES. PLEASE REPLY TO ME CARE OF FLETCHER MARKLE CBS NEW YORK CITY. VERY URGENT

NOXON, GERALD

70

[NEW YORK CITY]
[MID-APRIL 1947]

MALCOLM LOWRY
PHONE DOLLARTON P. O. DOLLARTON, B.C.
MANY THANKS ACCEPTANCE COLUMBIA OFFER STOP
PLEASE UNDERSTAND WE CANNOT DO ANYTHING LIKE JUS-
TICE TO BOOK ON RADIO STOP MORE LIKE A MOVIE TRAILER
BUT WILL DO OUR DAMNDEST TO PRESERVE INTEGRITY.
STOP VOLCANO GOING GREAT GUNS NEW YORK LOVE
GERALD

71

Front Street
Niagara-on-the-Lake
Ontario
May 9, 1947

Dear Malc and Margie:

Now that the excitement is over and I am back in a reasonable atmosphere of calm, I can write you the letter I should have written weeks ago,
but of which I found myself quite incapable. To begin with I don't know
whether you heard the broadcast or not, but to be on the safe side we had
a recording of the whole show made for you and it is now on its way up
from N. Y. In due course it will reach Vancouver where I shall make arrangements for you to hear it. I'm afraid it is not likely to rouse your enthusiasm for to me it was heartbreaking to have to operate with such
crudity on the book. From the radio point of view it was an excellent
show and has been acclaimed as such by all and sundry, but for anyone
acquainted with the book it was bound to be a disappointment. However,
the point is that the radio version reached a vast audience who would in
the ordinary way never have read the book at all, but who may now in
some instances go out and buy it. Anyway I'm sure it was well worth
doing and I was very happy that Columbia chose the *Volcano* for opening
their new series. The show and Markle got a tremendous burst of public-
ity in the New York Press, in *Time, Newsweek* etc. I send you a sample
advance notice from *PM*. Reviews of the show will follow as soon as
they reach me. As far as I was concerned, the best thing about the broadcast was Everett Sloane's performance as the Consul. You may remem-

ber him as the lawyer, Bernstein in *Citizen Kane,* a wonderful actor. Incidentally many people in N. Y. suggested that a stage version of the *Volcano* would be a good idea, and I think myself it could be done pretty effectively. What are your thoughts on it?

I met Erskine and Taylor while in N. Y. and liked them both, particularly Erskine who seemed the more perceptive of the two. As you probably know they are both at Random House now and seem pretty pleased about it. I did a round of some of the N. Y. bookstores to check up on *Volc* sales and found that it was selling very well and very steadily. However I guess you are in possession of all the information as to that. I must say it's really very heartening to know that a good book can sell so well without benefit of book clubs and with practically no advertising. I haven't seen a single ad for it since the early ones in the *Times Book Review.* Incidentally, have you seen the latest *Atlantic Monthly* — an excellent notice for the *Volcano,* really one of the best yet.

However, I daresay by now you are becoming rather bored with the whole subject and are busy with new things. As for my own activities, apart from approximately a month spent in N. Y. in connection with the broadcast, there is little to report. Some progress on "Clegg's Wall" but not enough I'm afraid to make it worth while my sending any to you. I do hope now to get down to it seriously.

We have rented this place for July and August and have taken a house on Martha's Vineyard for that period. I hope to be doing more work for Columbia during the summer and it will be handier to be a bit nearer N. Y. Here the snow has gone but the temperature remains that of winter with frost at night and the furnace still going full blast. Needless to say B and I are more than ready for some warmth. We have B's parents with us at the moment and they send their regards to you both. I expect you are basking in sunshine or at least in warm rain.

Many many thanks for the snaps which really did turn out well, particularly of Malc on the front steps which is one of the best of him I've seen. (Goodness how far behind I am in acknowledging same.) And incidentally after you left here, while B was in N. Y. a very persistent gentleman whom I took to be a representative of M. G. M. was trying hard to get Malc on the phone from Hollywood. I gave him all indications about how to reach you, but he was both incredulous and highly petulant when I informed him that you did NOT have a telephone. In the end, he growled something about you not being interested in $150,000 and rang off. His name was either Goldstein or Gluckstein or some such. I wonder whether he finally connected with you? A very horrible man over the phone, but I think he was out of temper at having to phone such an outlandish place as Niagara-on-the-Lake. They had probably told him that it didn't exist!

Nick is feeling very good because he got 75 in oral arithmetic—a miracle, in our opinion. Do write when you get the chance, either or both and let us know what goes on. Love to you both and happy days on the Inlet.

Yours ever,
Gerald

72

Front Street
Niagara-on-the-Lake
Ontario
May 25, 1947

Dear Malc:

A short note in behalf of a friend. Gilbert Harding whom you met briefly in Toronto has been a BBC representative in Canada for the last three years. The other day he received orders to return to England and on his arrival there he has every reason to believe that he will be politely but firmly sacked. They can do this because he was what they call a "war temporary." It's a very serious business for him because he's forty and has a mother to support etc. He read law and before the war was well on towards being called to the bar when things blew up. He thinks he would make a successful barrister and I agree with him, in fact it's quite obviously his metier and he has the right connections.

So what he wants to do when he gets back to England is to complete his law studies and become a barrister. In order to do this however he needs a thousand pounds which he hasn't got. He wants to borrow it and re-pay at the rate of a hundred a year plus interest on "note of hand alone."

I have a vague recollection that you said you had some money tied up in England which you couldn't get out of the country or otherwise employ. If this is the case, would you or could you consider making a loan to Harding? I fully realise I may have got this all wrong and there is no such "frozen cache." In which case please forget the whole thing. I wouldn't have bothered you with it except for the fact that I know Harding is going to be really up against it, and I want to do what I can to help him.

Here things go on much as usual. I'm making slow, but fairly steady progress with "Clegg" and will have some new chapters to send you before long. How goes your work? Write when you can, Malc.

Love to you both,
Gerald

73

Dollarton, B.C.
June 21, 1947

Dear Gerald:

—I feel very guilty not having written before but I assure you, as you once remarked some years back, it hasn't been possible within the last month.

And when it was I was hoping to get a letter from you, which might have made my P. S. so much longer than my letter that I put it off. Unless you can call the joint letter [see *Selected Letters,* May 1947] I wrote you and Fletcher a letter and now I think the word "letter" has been used enough, unless I should say that I must acknowledge both yours of May 9 and 25th.

Re the broadcast, thank you for the reviews, for much, and also thank you exceedingly for doing it. I have also received a quite ecstatic letter from Reynal & Hitchcock, or rather Reynal, or rather Kerr of R. & H. about it—and a very enthusiastic one from the *Daily Worker,* as also excellent reports from elsewhere. So far as I can gather it went off fine, I only hope you got some fun out of it, in spite of the hard work at such short notice—though we were hellishly disappointed not to hear it over the radio, this was unavoidable.

The recording you so kindly sent me got a bit delayed and when we did hear it it seemed it was not made quite deep (i. e. on the shellac) enough, though we got a good idea and enjoyed it: we liked it very much on the whole. Sloane's odd interpretation, everyone else to the contrary, was my chief criticism. I know he's a damn fine actor, but I cannot see why he emoted Lostweekendwise so much. He could have just *spoken* plenty of horrors, and poetry too, and it would have been more all right by me: but I guess I reckon without the difficulties.

Re Gilbert Harding: I am sorry to hear of his status and have been re-enquiring re mine in England: it would appear that my money is invested in such a way that I cannot draw any such sum as required out, nor could he even if I empowered him to do so, in England. What was owing to me retroactively was a different matter: but what is now invested has to remain in its present state of investment, I have no doubt a highly unwise one: but there seems little I can do about it, for I guess they now need it: in fact I expect to be borrowed from by them at any moment. For the rest, though I seem to be earning quite hard cash, I haven't even got my first royalty statement yet—taxes would suggest there is more in logging. I enjoyed your broadcast—including Harding's blague—I hope that wasn't what got him into trouble.

Hope you are working hard on "Clegg's Wall" and to hear more of this soon: we both have great hopes for "Clegg's Wall."

I am striving with a more than *Volcano,* and hard it is, but coming along: Margie has been having a spot of bother with the doctors, and I with my ears (my ear canals are apparently more suitable for a raven than a human being, at all events they go the wrong way) but we, apart from that, are well, swimming and in the old "rutiny" as Whitey would say—he sends regards.

Herewith my apologies re Harding—but dammit, he'll surely get on.

Re "Branches:" would you kindly, as a favour to me, dig out 6 or 7 of what you consider the best—maybe the sound of heavy things falling in the night—and send them to A. J. M. Smith, or on second thoughts, send them to *me,* since he's here now in Vancouver and I can reach him.

I know you are ticklish to approach on this subject and may think this bloody cheek on my part, but as I say I am asking you to do it as a favour and you can but say no, or if yes, should any result be toward, can refuse again.

If this doesn't reach you in Niagara, hope it does in Martha's Vineyard. Hope you are having a swell time there.

God bless and all the best love to yourself and Betty and Nick from both of us.

> su amigo
> l'oltre difficilissimo Malc

74

> Front Street
> Niagara-on-the-Lake
> Ontario
> June 25, 1947

Dear Malc:

Overjoyed to hear from you. I was beginning to get a bit worried in spite of myself. Damn silly and I really ought to know better, being world's champion at not writing when I ought to or how or what. As a matter of fact I feel that I owe you a letter somehow, since my last was just a duty note, a real shot in the dark so to speak. But I thought there was just a mere chance re Harding and felt compelled to do something. He'll probably fall on his feet all right, but I certainly don't envy him going back to G. B. right now. The crazy thing is that they should keep him here. In spite of, or probably because of his amazing English act and calculated rudeness, he's been the best man the BBC have ever sent here, only they're too dumb to know it. Anyway, thanks for thinking about it, Malc, and now forget it.

I'm glad you finally heard the recording of the show. They *were* very bad recordings and when Fletcher and I first heard them we were absolutely downcast. All the sound effects were missing, the music seemed ineffective and only Sloane's voice seemed to get across which threw the whole thing out of balance. Incidentally, about Sloane: you may be interested to know that Norman Corwin—he was here visiting us a few weeks ago—agrees with you entirely on the subject of Sloane's performance— just didn't like it at all. Myself, I find it hard to judge because the whole show seemed so dreadfully inadequate in relation to the book, and I find it impossible to consider it apart from the book. That difficulty however certainly didn't arise in the case of the average listener to CBS and thought of just as something to listen to on the radio, I guess it was O. K. And if the publishers liked it I suppose it served at least one useful purpose. I enjoyed doing it of course. I enjoyed the difficulty of doing it and regret only the fact that it was not better done. And all the time Fletcher and I were limp with sorrow that it wasn't a movie version we were working on. Incidentally have there been any developments in that direction?

You are working and that is good. So am I and quite furiously on "Clegg." I'm on the episode I call "Gisele" which deals with Clegg's unfortunate affair with French girl. It's a fairly big slab of the book and I hope to complete it in first draft while at Martha's Vineyard. We go there on July first for two months. Address: Quauk Cottage, Cedar Neck, Vineyard Haven, Mass. I'll send you "Gisele" to read whenever I get it in a legible state.

As for "Branches," I'm glad to send you those bits which you have seen before and on which I shall do no more work. There are others, new and old, but I am uncertain about them, am continually changing and revising them. I have of necessity to write so much rapid junk to earn money that I think it has made me pathologically jittery about these poems for which I care. In any case, as Smith has not seen any of them before, the ones familiar to you should serve the purpose. Some of the newer ones that you have not seen are approaching finality I think and you can be sure I'll send them along as soon as I think they're worth sending.

Conrad, we learn, is back in Brewster [on Cape Cod] while Mary holds the house that Jeake built [in Rye, Sussex], in hopes of selling same. We hope to see C. on our way to the Vineyard. God knows how he's going to manage without Mary and we can't quite make out why he's come back alone. On verra.

Nick is going to a camp somewhere up in the pre-Cambrian for a month and will join us later on the Vineyard. We have a house on the water with a boat which will make me think of you both. I do hope the canal troubles aren't serious and that nothing else of a medical nature is with you or Margie. I suppose you heard about Perkins of Scribner's — I mean that he is no more according to the papers. The publishing business seems altogether unsafe these days.

> All my love to you both
> Yours ever
> Gerald

75

FRONT STREET
NIAGARA-ON-THE-LAKE
ONTARIO
[SUMMER 1947]

MALCOLM LOWRY, FONE DOLLARTON P. O., DOLLARTON, B.C.
VOLCANO SUBJECT BOOK DISCUSSION ON CBC TRANS-CANADA NETWORK TOMORROW SUNDAY ELEVEN P.M. EDT SEVEN YOUR TIME I THINK STOP AM ON PROGRAM SELF AND WILL TRY TO PREVENT ANY TOO GROSS MISREPRESENTA-TION RE YOUR MOTIVES ETC. LOVE TO YOU BOTH.
> GERALD

76

Quauk Cottage
Vineyard Haven
Massachusetts
August 2, 1947

Dear Malc:

I said I'd send you a few more "Branches" when I was finished working on them. Here then are four which I don't think you've seen in any form before. They're a mixed bag as you will see. I'm not particularly happy about any of them. XIV & XV were originally written long ago but have undergone some comparatively important changes recently. XLI is a complete and recent re-write of another piece on the same theme. LX is new and really just an exercise in a style that I've been trying to perfect for a long time. There is quite a bunch more on the way now. I've had to abandon completely the more or less realistic framework I originally had in mind for "Branches," although the metaphysical scaffolding so to speak remains unchanged. Love to you both and let us hear from you when you can manage it,

Yours ever,
Gerald

LETTER 77

June 1948

In the fall of 1947 the Lowrys decided to spend the winter months in Europe. They left Vancouver in November and, after a rough passage, reached Le Havre in December. In Paris Lowry offered his assistance to the French translators of *Under the Volcano,* but was of little use: he was drinking constantly and could barely write his own name. When bouts of drinking mingled with murderous bouts of rage, Margerie had him hospitalized. However, in May 1948 the Lowrys were able to travel to Florence, and in June to Rome (where they delighted in tracing the path along the Via Nomentana taken by the characters in Noxon's novel, *Teresina Maria*) and Capri. It was not until January 1949—following Margerie's complicated but unsuccessful efforts to get Lowry to Switzerland to see Jung—that the Lowrys returned to Canada.

77

Rome
June 12, 1948

Dear old Gerald:

—Am here in your old stamping ground & we took a trip down the Via Nomentana in honor of Sig. Bicci & Teresina day before yesterday. How goeth "Clegg's Wall"? Your descriptions in *T. M.* seem awfully true. I like Rome excessively, however, far more than Paris & Margie's in her

7th heaven. We proceed not very originally if gaily to Capri to-morrow where our address is just Parma Posta. *Volc* is coming out in Italy soon: the publisher is the son of President & G'issimo. *Volc* was a flop in England, but apparently book-club etc. stuff in France. Best love from Margie and me to Betty Nick & yourself.

love

Malc

love

Margerie

LETTERS 78-80

January 1952 to Spring 1952

In January 1949, after the tumult of their fourteen-month European tour, the Lowrys returned to Dollarton, and Lowry settled down to some serious work on his short stories as well as "La Mordida" and *Dark as the Grave Wherein My Friend Is Laid*. However, he shortly learned that Frank Taylor, previously one of his editors of *Under the Volcano* in New York but now a producer with MGM in Hollywood, was interested in a good film treatment of F. Scott Fitzgerald's *Tender Is the Night*. After reading the novel himself, Lowry was convinced that he and Margerie should try their hand at adapting it for the screen. In the summer and fall Lowry became so absorbed in the project that it expanded to proportions which would have made it virtually impossible to film. He mailed the huge manuscript (455 pages in all, and resembling *Under the Volcano* as much as Fitzgerald's original) to Hollywood in April 1950. It was generally acknowledged as brilliant by all who dared read it—Frank Taylor, as well as James Agee, Jay Leyda, and Christopher Isherwood—but MGM had by then lost interest in the project.

In November 1951 Lowry wrote a lengthy, systematic statement in which he outlined in elaborate detail his long-standing plans to place all of his work—whether published or in progress—within the context of a multi-book project which he called "The Voyage That Never Ends." He submitted his "Work in Progress" outline to Robert Giroux at Harcourt, Brace—the firm which held the option on Lowry's contract after having bought out Reynal and Hitchcock. Giroux was initially enthusiastic about Lowry's project, but after several months (in March 1952) sent an apologetic letter to Lowry giving "financial considerations" as the reason for refusing to exercise the option on Lowry's contract. Lowry also sent a copy of his "Work in Progress" proposal to Albert Erskine at Ran-

dom House, where Erskine and his superiors were sufficiently impressed
to offer Lowry a contract and an advance.

Funds provided earlier by Harcourt, Brace enabled the Lowrys to
move to Vancouver for the winter of 1951-52; there they received word
(letter missing) from Noxon, who had moved to Boston in the late 1940s,
that he and Betty had divorced and that he had remarried. In his January
23, 1952 letter, Lowry makes reference to Gerald's new situation as well
as to an incident which must have occurred with regard to certain passages from Noxon's "Branches of the Night" manuscript. Lowry had
earlier asked Noxon to send him selections of the work to show to a publisher, and it seems as if Lowry failed in his efforts to help place those
pieces.

By now Lowry and Noxon had not seen each other for five years and,
though they did not know it, were not to see each other again. In his 1961
reminiscence Noxon gave his impressions of the last decade of Lowry's
life, from 1947 to 1957:

> Again, after the publication [of *Under the Volcano*], and after the
> radio version of the book had been done, broadcasts occurred, I
> heard only spasmodically from Malcolm and from many different
> parts of the world, it seemed: from France, from Italy, and finally it
> appeared that he had returned to England, which at one time he said
> that he would never do. One, of course, says those things but circum-
> stances alter cases and, in his case, the case was altered.
>
> Anyway, I saw nothing of him and I knew nothing of his later lit-
> erary efforts, although, of course, I fully expected our paths to cross
> again as they had done before. The last indication of a new book, that
> he told me all about when he was in Niagara in 1947, was a novel
> called "La Mordida," "The Bite," which was again a novel about
> Mexico. . . . What happened to "La Mordida" I don't know; I know
> some of it was written, sketches for part of it certainly were written.
> Whether this was lost or mislaid I have no knowledge at this time,
> but it seemed to me to have much more interesting possibilities than
> "In Ballast to the White Sea," the novel which was lost, destroyed
> in the fire. Frankly, I felt that ["In Ballast"] was . . . greatly inferior
> to the *Volcano* and in "La Mordida" I felt that he would continue in
> something of the same way as he had done in the *Volcano*.
>
> When I heard of his death, I was conscious of the fact that—of not
> a very great degree of surprise because, frankly, this might have hap-
> pened at almost any time, for many reasons. It was also with a feel-
> ing of profound shock, because I felt a writer of quite extraordinary

calibre had left the scene and that we would have no more from him.

On the other hand, I was conscious too, really, of the fact that we were lucky to get what we did; that in the *Volcano,* and in some of the shorter pieces, we had some masterly work which is in the great tradition of English writing and that we might easily have had none of it.

I was very fond of Malcolm, but he was a person who lived as he had to live and over whom one could have no more than a certain kind of an influence. He had to go his own way. He did go that way. And it was for him the only way. (Noxon, 1961)

78

1075 Gilford St.
Dantesque no. Apt. 33
Vancouver, B.C.
Canada
January 23, 1952

My poor beloved old Gerald:
I am appalled by what you tell me. I didn't know anything could hit me so hard either. And we couldn't understand it: when we wrote to Niagara, the letters were returned (I was trying to explain what had happened to the selections from "Branches," namely nothing, was not only not my fault but due to loyalty to yourself and "Branches" in the first instance, and untrustworthiness and carelessness and for all I know even professional jealousy on the part of another Canadian poet—(not A. J. M. Smith)—that I was foolish enough to trust, in the second—I had to, because we had to take a boat weeks earlier than we thought, but maybe all this will work out for the best in the end: still I figured you would have a right to blame me anyway, and in any case I felt you would have some cause to curse me and I was anxious to prove to you that this miscarriage was not due to any callousness in regard to "Branches," and certainly no lack of deep respect for the work, which was the only thing that mattered here as between you and me, because they probably wouldn't have printed it right or something anyway and I was sufficiently punished by their printing something of mine I gave no permission for)—Oh Jesus, Oh Montreal, my poor old Gerald. I guess that in some

ways I am such a malevolent character, or have in certain senses suffered so much myself, that I almost take sadistic pleasure in hearing that something has happened to so-and-so, or that such and such has suffered, or what, what-not has come to pass with Herr So und so: that may indeed be because I feel in some sort it serves them right or because, vile hermit, I love so few people myself. I don't like to think that this is true, and perhaps it really isn't. But whether or not, it certainly wasn't and isn't true here with you, for God's sake! No tithe of a ghost of satisfaction that my old companion's ship had hit a hurricane while mine was still riding pretty smoothly crossed my consciousness: no evil leer deformed or deforms one corner of my mouth while with the other I was or am pretending to be sorry. I am just horribly and agonizingly sorry, on every plane at once, that this has come to pass, & that you have had to suffer so much. Moreover I woke up to the fact that you are undoubtedly one of the best friends and indeed one of the only real friends I have—or we have—which simply makes it worse. We were so sad we left our 2 Christmas presents under the tree unopened and didn't open them. And in fact we haven't accepted it yet: it seems incomprehensible. I don't believe it, as you would say. Still, this is not the way to talk. We wish you all happiness in your new life with your wife, and happiness to her, and again and again to you both! We likewise have never ceased to think of you, always expect and look for your step on the rural stair, from time to time retrace the walks & the talks of a decade ago. Nothing is lost, nothing forgotten—not even your criticism of the madhouse story which I was working on when we received your news, and was just saying to myself: "H'm, this is where old Gerald said it was lousy, the protagonist shouldn't take 2 steps forward, and two steps backward, at least not *again*. He was quite right . . . " Everything is much the same, save we rebuilt the house as you know: and instead of the *Volcano,* there is *Lunar Caustic* and another volume of tales called *Hear Us Oh Lord From Heaven Thy Dwelling Place.** (But because Hitchcock died and Reynal merged into Harcourt, Brace, to whom I was then bound, and my editor went to Random House, and the pound went down, and no stories were accepted by magazines (by either of us, alack) and one could get no money out of Europe, save after endless red tape, we have had a hell of a time slugging it out the last 3 years, sometimes on less than $80 a month, (I broke my back too in a fall from the pier, somehow recovered with no ill consequences). The winters have got as cold as Niagara here and once or twice—with our cardboard inside walls and no heater—we've damn nearly frozen to death; this is not just a figure of speech. It has happened several times in other shacks further down. The typewriter likewise froze both this winter and the winter before last and once we didn't take our clothes off for weeks. The first time I have ever really encountered the SPECTRE at first hand, I guess. This time I swore I'd get Margie out into an apartment for the winter and *Hear Us Oh Lord* was accepted just before Christmas, they wired us an advance—and somehow, between the Canadian Pacific Telegraph Co and our bloody postmaster in Dollarton,—we didn't get the wire for a week. Something like what happened with the hundred bucks you sent for Margie. What really puts the double whammy on the irony is that the bloody postmaster, who is as you remember also the storekeeper, was dunning us to pay our bill to him while calmly sending back the money that was arriving for us. How much mail or cash or opportunities we may have lost we simply don't know. But I don't think he'll do it again. Shades of Kafka! This winter we just sat and shivered until the advance came. Well, it was an emergency advance on an advance, which made it all the worse to have it delayed. By which time it was too late to get an apartment for the winter in Vancouver, but we finally have: *no. 33,* good luck:—Dantesque number as I said, and Margie is delighted with it, and we shall work here till April, commuting from time to time to Dollarton (where we nearly got wiped out altogether too—like they feared would happen with old St. Petersburg,—in a freak high tide, with a continuing easterly gale)—pardon all this.)

I don't understand the bit where you say that you guessed you had it coming to you. In fact I can't even guess at the "it." I have always admired the way you grappled practically with this world and the guts you showed in regard to your responsibilities—certainly not easy when a creative artist, and the mode of grappling not sufficiently off center to art not to tempt you away from creating altogether; I can't think of a harder problem, especially when you always have the creative artist within one to say: But what about your responsibilities to *me?* And it had seemed to me that you were nobly on your way to solving it—even to make the tangential and necessary activity serve you. You speak of guts being taken out and replaced—do you speak figuratively, or psychoanalytically. Explain, or not, as you wish. Say little, much, or nothing. But whatever it is don't blame yourself too hard. Even Carlson steered too far north (and then found he couldn't steer at all, but in fact that may have been the ship's fault).

And in all senses, a new birth, and happiness to you both from us. How goes Nick?—Best love to him. With great love from us both.

Malc

Send news of *Teresina,* "Clegg's Wall," "Branches," —job; —hold that note, Roland!

* after the Manx fisherman's hymn. Longest story is about fishermen in Dollarton & our life there. Several others are Canadian stories, & one, about a Liberty ship that loses her steering gear in cyclone approaching Scillias—practically same place as Enterprise & personal experience of ours, must have scared publishers stiff over New Years, since I haven't heard from them since they accepted book.

—About 14 months ago I wrote Einaudi in Torino dedicating Italian translation of *Volcano* to you (without your permission since I couldn't seem to get in touch) & Margie: but have received no reply. Evidently they have delayed the translation: perhaps they did not get the letter, but whether or no please take the will for the deed; the more especially since the deed was did from this end.

79

[1075 Gilford Street
Apt. 33
Vancouver, B.C.
Canada
January 23, 1952]

Darling old Gerald—

Your news made us quite sick. We can't get used to it, or get over it, or understand it. You know I loved you both very dearly. —and Nick, I try to think of him all, or almost, grown up now, but I still "see" him, at Oakville, "disappearing into the sun." Give him my love. Oh Gerald, for Jesus sake man! this is all too bloody awful. But with all my heart I wish you happiness & a new start. Please give your wife all my very best wishes for everything. My God I wish we could see you!

Love,
Margerie

80

Dollarton, B.C.
Canada
[Spring 1952]

—Time for the train that "goes a long way," i. e., toward Port
Moody and points east . . . *y'lang, y'lang.*

Beloved old Gerald:

This written in haste and in a state of gnattering partly because of a
high temperature: first Margie with the spring fever, now me, the
weather bloody and Dollarton half smashed up last winter (though our
"gazebo" as you called it, the pier, as does our house, still stands,
nobly, though I say it who ought not, or ought, since one lives in it: and
it still is, as always, waiting for your spring visit, blaze of primroses as
you once said still there, same primroses, though that same house is not
there, except for that old semi-woodshed outside of which you used to
sit, now part of the new house, shit on this prose). Immediate trouble
though is a debt, albeit one of honor, incurred by me or us to one Albert
Erskine, Random House, 457 Madison Ave., New York 22.

This debt (I mean the debt that I have morally to pay in a hurry) is precisely to the tune* of that which you were good enough to inform us that
owing to the default of our postmaster, you owe to us, or rather Margie:
and it would make us sleep better, if you have it, or even if you
don't—sleep better not on your account but on ours—if having it, or having it not, you were able to send this amount to the said Erskine, reason
being that the said good Erskine, likewise stuck with difficulties of
divorce and above that of teeth, lent us this money out of what he had
reserved to pay his dentist.

Fate moves in a mousterious way, as Bobbie Burns did not care to
remind his field mouse, who now occupy our entire quarters from garden
to roof to basement, which was the bear's cage, as you remember: when
not suffering from delirium tremens one should encourage them to eat
wild bleeding heart and chickweed rather than one's dinner, though we
haven't the bleeding heart to kill one yet, not even with mousecide.

When I have told you this I have not told you all; principally that I believe Random House and the Modern Library—of which the said Albert
Erskine (whom you remember) is now the managing editor—are now, after long and agonized wrangling, my publishers: they aren't going to give
me a big advance, however, but a small sum every month for the next
few years to enable me to get some work completed; this makes it diffi-

cult to pay out lump sums. But this is an immediate matter of teeth, Erskine's teeth: and must be paid back to him, somehow, by summer.

Meantime the *Volcano* has been a smash hit in Germany and there was even talk of making a movie of it there con Peter Lorre; they sent me a contract months ago offering me fifty-fifty; I refused (even though broke) unless I—we**—could have a say in the script, haven't heard any more but the fact remains that—

> God bless you,
> from us both to you both
> Malc

* i.e. $100.

** & even, the faint hope persisted, perhaps you?

P.S. I left out the most important part. Since it now seems that a long term contract is definitely going through with Random House I should—though not immediately, for we have to get out of debt first—be eventually in a position where, should you be short at anytime, we could lend you a spot of dough. We haven't forgotten your great generosity in lending us that 200 when we got burned out not to say generosity in other respects. I couldn't thank you too much for the help you gave me with the *Volc* & Margie with the *Horse* & we only wish to God we were lucky enough to have your counsel at the moment in regard to Work in Progress. Hope you are well & happy, all the best to Nick, & love to your wife & self.

> Malc

INDEX

Noxon, Nicolas (Betty and Gerald
Noxon's son), 8, 49, 52, 60, 85, 93,
94, 100, 102, 104, 106, 111, 114, 130,
133, 137, 140, 143, 147, 155, 156
Noxon, William C. (Gerald Noxon's
father), 13, 67, 70

Our Canada (Joe), 16, 37, 51

"Paradiso." *See* "In Ballast to the White
Sea."
Parks, Benjamin, 6
Pelleas and Melisande, 96, 97
Percy. *See* Cummins, Percy.
Perkins, Maxwell, 128, 147
Pilgrim's Progress, The, 119
Pillars of Hercules, 82
PM, 141
Point of Honor, The, 71
"Port Swettenham," 12
Private Snuffy Smith, 42
Prokofieff, Sergei, 42
Proust, Marcel, 134
Puccini, Giacomo, 80
Pudovkin, Vsevlod I., 12, 33

Racine, Jean, 83
Ragging the Scale, 82
Random House, 69, 142, 151-52, 154,
157, 158
Ray, Man, 12
"R. B." *See* Empson, William.
Redburn, 58
Redes, 32
Redgrave, Michael, 25, 27
Renoir, Jean, 33
Retail Bookseller, 125
Reynal and Hitchcock (publishing
company), 117, 120, 121, 122, 123,
126, 135-37, 144, 151, 154
Richards, I. A., 5, 48
Richards' Bill. *See* Empson, William.
Rimbaud, Arthur, 44, 47
River, The, 32
Romances, 58
Romney, George, 134
Room, Alexander, 32, 35

St. Louis Blues, The, 51
Sam (neighbour of Lowrys at Dollarton),
2, 108

Schuster. *See* Simon & Schuster.
Scribner, Charles, 128
Scribner's, 58, 61, 69, 72, 105, 111, 123,
125-26, 128, 147
Secret Agent, The, 71
Secret Sharer, The, 71
Selected Letters of Malcolm Lowry, 2, 3,
5, 117, 144
Shadow Line, The, 71
Shaftesbury Avenue Pavilion Cinema
(London), 12
Shakespeare, William, 30
Shapes that Creep, The, 4n, 56, 58, 61,
123, 125
Shelley, Percy, 70-71
Simon & Schuster, 55, 105, 111, 113
"Skylark, The," 70-71
Sloane, Everett, 141-42, 144, 146
Smith, A. J. M., 145, 154
Song of Ceylon, The, 127
Spectator Short Films (London), 14
Spender, Stephen, 44, 46
Stage, 17
Stansfeld-Jones, Charles (magician), 2,
56, 59-60
Stern, James, 36
Stevenson, Robert Louis, 84, 130
Stong, Phil, 61
Storm Over Asia, 32, 82
Story Press, 28
Strand, Paul, 32
Street, The, 34
Studio One, 18
Sunrise, 127
Sunshine Sketches of a Little Town, 17,
110
Sykes-Davies, Hugh, 25, 27, 28

Taylor, Frank, 4, 142, 151
Tender Is the Night, 16, 151
ten Holder, Clemens, 4
Teresina Maria, 4n, 14, 16, 20, 53, 55,
56, 60, 62, 64, 68, 69, 70, 72, 74, 75,
76-83, 97, 101, 105, 111, 114, 118,
130, 132, 149, 156
They Fly for Freedom, 16, 37
"Thief in the House, A," 17
Time, 42, 132, 141
Times Book Review, 142
T. M. See *Teresina Maria.*
Tolstoy, Leo, 30